THE MOTORMAN'S DAUGHTER

SARAH MAC DONALD

BOMBSHELTER PRESS
Los Angeles / 2012

Copyright © 2012 Sarah Mac Donald
All rights reserved

Other than brief quotations in a review, no part of this book may be reproduced without written permission of the publisher or copyright holder.

ISBN: 978-0-941017-98-5

Bombshelter Press
www.bombshelterpress.com
books@bombshelterpress.com
PO Box 481266 Bicentennial Station
Los Angeles, California 90048 USA

Printed in the United States of America

All photographs copyright © 2012 Fae Horowitz www.faehorowitz.com
Layout & design: Alan Berman

DEDICATION

*To my two children,
Jordan and Jennifer Schwartz,
who have put up with me
for all of these years.*

ACKNOWLEDGEMENTS

I'd like to acknowledge the help of the following people, who have been there for me in many ways: Rev. Gabri Ferrer; William L. Wallace, Ph.D.; Fae Horowitz; Al Linton; Charles Arjavac; Richard Taylor; Michael Stroud; Stephanie Jourdan; Laura Israel; Milette Elicano, M.F.C.; Sumner I. Goldstein, M.D.; Trudy Goodman and the sangha of Insight L.A.; Jack Grapes and the Thursday morning class; Diane Rose and The Namaste Women's Choir; and most of all, my teachers, especially Mrs. Wiggenhorn, who, on a cold day in January, in a classroom at Goshen Central High, asked me how I was, and I told.

CONTENTS

Dedication III
Acknowledgements V

NOW

Here in Paradise 15
My Half Life 16
Latin for the Motorman's Daughter 18
There for the Taking 19
Who Would I Be If I Could? 20
Birdsong 21
Disappointment 22
Afternoon Tea 25
The Space Between 28
Cleopatra's Barge 30
The Narrow Path 31
Bukowski 33
To Be Fabulous 35
The Nectar of the Gods 36
The Silver Bracelet 38
The Mockingbird 40
The Touching Pool 41
Ouroboros, or the Snake That Ate Her Tail 49
My Garden 50
Enlightenment 52
One Day of Fall 53
Intelligence 54
Changes 55
Consolation of a Wasteland 56
Lines 57
The Train 58
May 23, 2010 59
Pretty Girl 61
My Personal Saint 62

Partly Cloudy, Mostly Sunny. 63
When Worlds Collide 65
The Street. 66
The Old Black and White Dog. 69
The Frozen Child. 71

THEN

When I Was Small 75
The Sea Monsters 76
Don't Tell 79
Aunt Sis. 81
Jesus Loves Me 83
The Surprise 85
Mother Love 88
Rachel 90
The House of Secrets 92
Sonny 94
The Cold Pool 95
Scavenger 96
Old Tom. 98
Uncle Dick 99
Uncle Lloyd 100
Witness 102
Sarah 104
Grandma 105
The Mark. 107
Advice. 108
The Frozen Child. 109
My Life 111
Mother. 112

THE FLIPPING WIDOW

My One and Only. 115
The Flipping Widow 117
My Kitchen. 118
Marvin. 119

A Widow Dreams 120
Tomatoes 121
Six Months after Marvin's Death 122
The Silver Elephant 123
His Death, the Buddhists and Me 124
His Death, the Christians and Me 126
It's Been a Year—Almost 127
Yahrzeit 129

AN ASSEMBLAGE OF POETS

Jane Kenyon—I 133
Jane Kenyon—II 134
A Letter to All of Them, but Mostly to Jane 135
Jane and the Poet 137
Penultimate Letter to Jane 138
Why It's Time for Me to Say Goodbye
  to Jane, Hayden, Yevgeny and Anna 139
Sergei Yesenin—I 140
Sergei Yesenin—II 141
To Donald Hall 142
Jim Harrison 143
Leaving Jane 144
Me, Jane, Gus and Gracie 145

FROM NOW & THEN ON

The Visitor 149
Vacation 151
Windows 152
All the News That's Fit to Print but Who Wants to Read It? 153
The Path 156
The Crows 157
The City 158
Dreams 159
The Boys 160
A New Day 161
The Big Red Dog 162

The Splitter-Upper	163
Sunday Morning	171
The Beginning	172
Gracie	173
Solace	174
Small Things	175
October 20, 2010	176
Love Story	177
The Demon Mirror	178
A Lamentation	180
Lovers	182
Last Lover Poem	183
Joining the Orange Butterfly	184
A Weekday Morning	185
A Walk in the Fog	186
A Strange Day	187
A Blue Moon Day	188
A Happening	189
By Heart	190
During a Meditation	191
Failed Promises	192
My Muse	193
Rimbaud Squared	194
My Mind	195
Potential	196
A Friday in January	197
Valentine's Day 2011	198
The Garden	199
The Whole Truth	201
The Showing	204
Storage	207
Palliative	208
My Table	209
Home	210

The Motorman's Daughter

We shall not cease from exploration
And the end of all our exploring
Will be to arrive where we started
And know the place for the first time.

T.S. Eliot, "Little Gidding"
from *Four Quartets*

NOW

*Cloquet hated reality,
but realized it was
the only place to
get a good steak.*

Woody Allen, "The Condemned"

Here in Paradise

April is the cruelest month, but not in California.
Here one month bleeds into another.
There is no guide, no marking of our days,
the weather comes and goes
talking of Michelangelo.
The only thing we notice is earthquakes
and we don't talk of them.
We all know about earthquake weather.
That's when it's hot and smoggy
and our skin hurts.
That's when we crack.
That's when the earth breaks.
We do not talk of it.

The ocean is red, the ocean is on fire.
Water can burn.
It's not the sky that will kill us.
It's what happens in the depths.

The dying ocean, the dying turtle
and the dying sea bird.
They are one.
One being each one.
Death in the particular.
Who cares about groups?
Look at each one.
Look at me dying a little each day.

There are no death days.
There are no death seasons.
There are no death holidays.
Death can come anytime.
From below,
from above,
from afar,
dressed like a hipster or a checker in a market.
It's hard to see him, here in paradise.
We mark our days by season finales.

My Half Life

Sometimes I feel as though I'm trapped in a fairy tale called "The Wild Swans" by Hans Christian Anderson. It's about a young girl, a princess, with eleven brothers and a wicked stepmother. The stepmother is so jealous that she puts a spell on the brothers and turns them into swans. The little princess wants to save her brothers and the only way to do this is by weaving coats out of nettles, which are very painful to work with and cause her hands to blister. She also must be silent while she is doing the weaving. She keeps silent and weaves until she is almost burned at the stake for being a witch, and at the last minute, flings the coats over her brothers and they all become men again, except for the youngest. Because she hasn't been able to finish, one of his arms remains a swan's wing.

In my version of that fairy tale, most of the time I'm the princess, except instead of weaving coats, I'm condemned to write, and at the same time, I have to keep silent. Because of this conflict, each word that comes out is associated with pain. That's why I write so sparingly—each word hurts and each word has to fight for its own existence.

I don't sit here easily. I'm not charmed by my own words. I'm embarrassed. I hate to read them back. They're not mine. They've forced themselves out of me. They bark at me in my left ear and squeeze themselves out of my fingers. I don't know why it has to be this way, but it is. I must keep silent and I must write.

What will happen if I don't write? Sometimes I feel that the world, which is already spinning out of control, will just erupt in flames; sometimes I feel that nothing will happen, that I've cast this spell on myself and if I finally speak, I will just bore myself to death or at least fall into a deep sleep.

My other take on this tale is that I am really the youngest brother, the one who didn't get the full coat, the one whose arm is that of a swan. That's why my right arm is crooked. It's not crooked because of a birth injury; it's still under a spell and has remained a swan's wing.

This makes a lot of sense to me since I've certainly run into a lot of wicked stepmothers and stepfathers in my life who have been very free with their spells. There are good things about this too. The arm doesn't hurt and it reminds me of who I am: part swan, part princess.

The one thing I do know is that I like living this half-life, this between-life. The one in which, when you close your eyes and look away, everything is different. The one where real living is done in sleep. The one where animals can talk and you can be greeted by the gods of the house when you come home.

Latin for the Motorman's Daughter

I have fallen in love with Latin again,
with Latin words—*miserere nobis, Deo gratias,*
Agnus Dei, pax vobiscum.

I studied Latin in high school.
It was supposed to be good for me, a classical education.
Appropriate for the motorman's daughter,
who knew all the stops on the IRT
and rode the Dinky to school.

The teacher talked of declining verbs.
Decline—what does that mean?
Present indicative—I'd like to decline
you touching my breast.
Subjunctive—I would rather
you take your hand out of my pants.
Pluperfect—it would have been pluperfect
If you'd have gotten the hell out of here.

I memorized it all—*amo, amas, amat.*
all her words had different meanings to me.
Who loves me? Does he love me?
Does anyone love me?
But there was no perfect in my life, much less pluperfect.
I wasn't loved. I hadn't been loved.
I would not ever have been loved.

I learned it all.
I learned to decline verbs
And roll myself into a ball when someone touched me.

I learned the indicative of touch,
The perfect of grope,
The subjunctive of fondle,
The pluperfect of stroke.
All in Latin,
perfect for the motorman's daughter.

There for the Taking

Yes, that's right, there is no time, no time, not a nanosecond.
No time for luscious, dripping, oozing sex.
No time for aroused nipples, hard cocks.
No time for lazing in bed waiting for the next
erection or the next licking or sucking
in the rumpled, damp sheets soiled with sex.

Yeah, that's all gone, gone in the ether, in the wind.
It's left in beds all over the world. I think Hawaii
was the best bed, then I remember France and Norway.
And I debate myself as I stimulate myself.
I was lush, there for the taking, mostly a kind word would suffice.

Those times, those in-between times, those silent, secret
wild times, those sacred times, those beloved times
are all there at the turn of a corner or the blink of an eye.
I looked into my lover's eyes and saw dark brown pools
of thick chocolate that I could lap and lick up with my tongue.

I also saw that he couldn't see them, he couldn't see his luscious
chocolate eyes. They were mine alone to see. I could see him
like a lover and I saved him in my brain and eyes and vagina
so that on a partly cloudy, windy coldish day in California
I could remember and glimpse that one beautiful eye that's mine alone.

Who Would I Be If I Could?

I used to dream of being a movie star.
June Allyson was my favorite:
the shy, pretty girl next door.

Nothing glam, nothing outrageous.
The type of girl who grows on you.
Best friends, once you open your eyes.

A wallflower.
Someone you hardly notice,
but who was always doing the right thing.

Always wearing a blue sweater
with a Peter Pan collar and fake pearls
and short white gloves, when appropriate.

The dream became a nightmare.
I got too big to be demure
and talked too much, forgetting to smile,
and I didn't like living next door to anyone.

Now I am the widow next door
with three birch trees and one small dog,
the widow who sits in her back room and looks at her creeping fig.

Birdsong

Outrageous sun, foolish bird singing,
oblivious to the world's spinning,
full of earthquakes, volcanoes and terrorists.
There is a cold wind blowing, coming from the heated desert,
spewing from the mouths of ignorant banal spirits.
Birdsong becomes tweets. Prayers are postings.
Kyrie Eleison. There is no Christ. No mercy.
It's all online. Texts from God.
Our mythology is binary. No room for the three-in-one.
Fahrenheit 451 is obsolete. Books died in cyberspace.
There is no place. Nothing is real.
There's nothing to get hung about.
Nothing from the Void.
Nothing from Non-being.
Nothing from NO-thing.
Tweet Tweet go
The Nothing birds,
The Nothing world,
The Nothing God.
Nothing to hold on to—nothing to carry around.
Nothing to lose, or find again, after many years lost.

Disappointment

I am acquainted with disappointment.
My lover came to me in a dream last night.
We danced, kissed, rubbed noses.
He left.

I have to find the words myself.
The words that will let me keep living.
Words full of self-solace that stop me
from giving up.

In my garden I have no one.
No one disappearing.
The flowers wither and die.
The blackbirds continue their migration.

Joey and Gracie will get old and die.
I will be alone again.

I have no more tears.

I've never been quite good enough.
Always an also-ran.
Not quite good enough.

Life in my garden is small and sure.
Pests can be sprayed away or stepped on
if you're not a Buddhist.

My dream is to stay here
surrounded by flowers, bugs and dogs.
No more lovers.

Nothing feels as empty as when a lover leaves.
I've learned how to talk myself into keeping going.
It will be better tomorrow.
I'll be better tomorrow.

He had bad grammar.
Couldn't pick out a tie.

Liked baseball. Hated cats.
Didn't love me.

I write of a lover as a man
but it could be a woman.
He could be a she.
I'm sure I'd love a woman.
Unless the lover is a mean bitch
that no one else wants.

A man walks on the dirt path
white cane in hand,
wearing a yellow shirt and blue jeans.
He walks straight up and down in a brisk rhythm.

You've got to know how to love yourself,
if you're in the land of the second-best.

The birches are active,
responding to the wind.
The birds are noisy.
I can hear a mockingbird in the distance.
I am happy sitting here writing, hearing the birds,
feeling the breeze.
My heart beats to its mad rhythm.
Syncopated like a bossa nova.

I hear the children play.
I can just see the bright fuchsia
of an optimistic geranium
near my front window.

A sparrow hops at the foot of my stately birches,
content to be looking for bits of food.
A squirrel chirps in the background
busy with his hunt.

I am happy sitting here writing,
hearing the birds,
feeling the breeze,
my heart bumping in its own mad rhythm.

The sparrow, the squirrel and I
share this little bit of time together.
Each on his own hunt. Content.

Everyone is neatly in his place,
including me, the listener,
the recorder, the prayer.
The insignificant one.
So much is given to me.
Every day is blessed.
All I have to do is breathe.
My heart has to remember to beat.

That's all.

Afternoon Tea

It was Tuesday afternoon and the dogs and I were sitting around the house. I had just finished reading *Northanger Abbey* for the fifth time and I was thinking of having some tea. The day was partly cloudy and the four o'clock wind had just come up from the beach so there was a chill in the air. The doorbell rang and the dogs ran to the door, barking. I opened the door and standing there, nicely dressed with a real Panama hat and an old-school tie, was an elephant.

"Hello," I said. I've always had a fondness for elephants.

He said, "May I come in?"

I welcomed him into my home and showed him to my living room, seating him on my shabby-chic green couch which I thought would handle his bulk rather well. The dogs lay down on either side of him.

"My name is Theodore," he said, "and I've come a long way to see you." He wiped his bow with a big white handkerchief.

"Would you like some tea?" I said. "I was just about to make some."

"I'd be very grateful," said Theodore. "I'm a little parched."

Since I live in Los Angeles, I have a lot of teas and he settled on Fleur de Geisha, an aromatic green one. He declined the pastries. "I'm watching my weight," he said. He did accept a few almonds. I had no peanuts to offer him.

We sat across from each other. I had baroque music playing in the background and I waited for him to speak.

After a few sips, he said "Sarah, may I call you that?" I nodded. "As I said, I've come a long way to see you. Since retirement, I've been living in Florida, where, except for the hurricanes, the climate is quite conducive to my well-being, as are the 'early bird' specials.

"I've been working a twelve-step program and I'm on step nine, which, as you may know, is the one in which I'm to make direct amends to whomever I've hurt wherever possible, except when to do so would injure them or others. I'm here to make amends to you."

I was shocked. "What amends?" I said. "I'm sure I would have remembered seeing you."

"It was a long, long time ago, when I was a little fellow," he said. "I had just started accompanying my mother to her job. We were with a traveling circus. That's when I met you."

A traveling circus, elephants, I thought. Then it hit me. When I was about five or six years old, Uncle Joe, Mom and Dad had taken me to Madison Square Garden to see the Ringling Brothers Barnum and Bailey Circus. It was a very big deal in my young life.

"I remember," I said. "There were a lot of lights and pretty women in fancy clothes and men flying in the air. I loved the horses and I didn't like the lion tamer because he used a whip. I liked the dog tricks, but I was a little iffy about the clowns. Mom loved the one who was sweeping the light."

"Yes, that's it. That's where it happened," he said.

"I remember having a lot of fun," I said. "I loved cotton candy and the peanuts. We saw the big show and I saw the bearded lady and the tall man and the little woman. I wouldn't go into the room where the lady wrapped snakes around her body. Then we went to see the animals that were resting between shows."

And then I remembered—the elephants. The elephants. I had seen them earlier in the parade and there was a cute little one holding onto his mother's tail. "Yes," I said. "We saw the elephants eating and drinking water out of tin pails when, out of the blue, the little one sprayed me with water. I got really soaked and I started to cry. It's a good thing Dad and Uncle Joe had big white handkerchiefs."

"That was me," said Theodore. "I did it. I sprayed you with water. I did it."

"Why?" I said.

"Well, I was a little tyke at the time and so were you. You seemed so nice and so little, like me, and I was really happy to see you. I thought you'd like a little cooling off like I did and I sprayed you with water. I really liked you and I didn't want to upset you."

"You did it because you liked me?" I said.

"I liked you and I saw you cry and I've always felt bad about you crying and I wanted to let you know that I'm sorry if you felt bad or misunderstood my actions."

"But everyone laughed at me. No one understood."

"I know, and I'm really, really sorry."

So there it was. A big moment in my life, full of laughter and humiliation, and he was really honoring me and saying hello. Wow. Despite that incident, I had always liked elephants, particularly Pooh's

Heffalump and Dumbo.

"I forgive you," I said. "Thanks so much for coming all the way out here, across this big country, after all these years. I forgive you." I went over to him to give him a hug and a big kiss on his leathery cheek.

He stayed a little longer. He told me tales of his career in the circus and how he was enjoying his retirement. He had recently started painting and was enjoying some success.

He stood up to go. I walked him to the door. The dogs and I stepped out to the sidewalk with him. I kissed him again and we watched him lumber off, his Panama hat firmly on his head, his tail twitching and swaying with his movement as he started up the hill on his way to the airport.

The Space Between

May 24th, 2009. Cloudy and overcast. It's cool out and my hands and feet are a little cold, but I don't want to take the time to stop to put on a robe. I'm in my favorite flannel pj's with the dogs on them. The bird in the yard is singing his head off.

It pisses me off that Proust might be right about "the remembrance of things past." Life is only good on the rewind. I'm thinking of Joni Mitchell—"Don't it always seem to go / that you don't know what you've got till it's gone."

I only want to write what's true about me right now, listening to the Baroque show on a cool Sunday morning with the bird singing in my backyard. The rhythm of the music comes to my left hand and left foot. A plane flies overhead and I can still hear the bird and the music.

I write. I keep writing. It's never right. It's never finished. I'm not very good. I'm pissed at myself because I'm not good enough. I'm not good and yet I keep on writing. It's aggravating to keep on doing something you're not really good at.

What is good? The truth is good. The bird song is good. Baroque music is good. The dogs are good. Creating the heavens and the earth is good. Resting on the seventh day is good.

I like writing because I can do it by myself and I don't need anyone to do it with. It's good to be alone. To stop. To mark. To take note of.

I saw a TV show while working out at the gym yesterday. In a public open house they planted a hidden camera in the living room to get people's comments as they walked through. Then they played it for the homeowner who was trying to sell the house. The comments were: "I feel like I'm in a funeral home." "This place is right out of the '70s." "It's dark and tacky." When they played it to the homeowner she said: "Nobody ever told me it was dark and tacky." Well, who would? Maybe I should have. I'm interested in the space between people. The space between us can be huge, as vast as the space between planets. If we get too close, the gravitational pull can tear us apart. No one ever says what they really think or what they really mean. The few times in my life that I've done so, I've regretted it.

I was in my twenties at a dinner party among friends and one guy was telling us how great everything was and how good he was feeling and how wonderful life was. I blurted out: "That's all right, honey. It won't last."

Everyone laughed. I didn't mean to be cruel. I didn't mean to be funny. I wasn't looking for a laugh. Everyone thought it was hysterical. I was embarrassed. The last I heard of him was that he had committed suicide by jumping off a building. Well, I was right. It didn't last. Nothing lasts. Joey is dying. Gracie's getting old. I'm becoming my mother with a wrinkled face.

So I write for no reason. For no good reason. Markings. Hammarskjold. Twain. I mark my life. I note it. I don't understand it. I don't celebrate it. I endure it. It is getting smaller each year. But I will always have music.

The bird still sings. The dogs nose around the garage looking for my husband. They match brown and white, mostly white. The same size. The dogs watch our lives. They are an undercurrent. The baseline of our days. Ready, always ready, for food or play and on guard for interlopers.

The sun is coming out. The sky is bluing and the music ends for now.

Cleopatra's Barge

I don't sit in the lap of fame.
No one's made a movie of my life.
I don't have my own boat in the Florida Keys,
and yet, I'm still here
for no good reason.

I've done my time.
I've messed up too many times to count.
Disappointed the world and myself.
Took the wrong turns.
Came up empty, dry, sere.
I never found rewind.
I am near the end,
working in a small house with a small dog.

I'm too old for love—for that gentle touch.
That smile across the room that the TV says
can happen at any moment.
Not to me. I have left the land
of fucking, except with myself, at night in the dark.

I have no dream lover.
No one for sharing my bed.
I am contained as a barge,
or an oil liner
filled with fuel
headed slowly down the shore.

The Narrow Path

Buddha, Kwan Yin, Julian,
silence, compassion, comfort,
plagues, pestilence, eruptions—
all here. Jostling our sentiments.
We scramble and sit on the silver Swiss ball,
silencing ourselves, dreaming of past times,
knowing that nothing, no thing has changed.
There is only one end to this story
that started at our birth.

The lake was shimmering in the moonlight.
There was a silver path to the moon.
We watched, my friend and I, on a summer's eve.
We watched as the woman dove in,
splashless, slicing the water.
We watched as she swam
following the silver path.
We three were there, together in the dark.
She was swimming for us and for the moon.
The professor's wife, caressing the water.
We watched on that still night, sensing beauty,
not knowing that she would be dead by winter.

I miss my friends, the ones I loved and hated.
I miss Paulie, who never grew.
I miss Laura Altrowitz, who wore thick glasses.
And Jimmy Bernhart, who was fat and funny.
We were so close, tramping on each other's shadows.
Elsa, who ate eel for lunch,
and Benjy who was a tattle-tale.
I miss them all, every one, and I never want to see them again.

My creeping fig has been trimmed.
It no longer touches the roof line.
A temporary haircut—that plant loves the roof.
I trim myself every day and walk the narrow path.
the narrow path around the lake
that waits for all of us.
I swim now for all of us,

the narrow path,
the silver path
to the moon.

Bukowski

It happened on Thursday. I dragged my fat old ass back into my writing class after about a year of not writing. The class was still being held in that square room with yellow walls and the wallpaper bookshelves. I got there early to get settled in. If I can, I always pick the red straight back chair so I can get out easily. I'd need a crane to haul me out of one of the couches.

They all showed up—an assembly of the usual suspects, mostly good looking younger people, peppered by older ones who've been in the business for a while and a few outlanders, like me. They're all mostly actors, who love words. They're dressed hip/smart/casual with a bohemian accent as only the folks in the City of Angels can do. All of them good-looking and eons younger than me. We sat around the big man, Jack, in a circle. A circle in that room with Jack at the almost center. What I don't get are the people who sit behind him—the ones content to listen to his words, not see his eyes.

Jessie also showed up. The big blonde greeter. She swooped into the room looking for food and settled down in her bed for a snooze.

I told my writing teacher what I wanted to do this time and read an unfinished, half-assed piece that I'd written. I hate standing up there naked with my boring story hanging out. Jack gave me a muse—Bukowski. And he said: "Don't get into any drunken bar fights."

Yeah, great Jack, thanks.

So, right after class, after three hours of listening to people pour out their hearts and guts, after listening to people who were witty and quick with words, after listening to people write elegant prose that would make Osama and Obama cry, listening, knowing that I was an outsider, faker, interloper, someone who would never make it, I took myself to Dutton's bookstore and went to the Bukowski section. Shit. That man wrote a ton of stuff. I bought a few books, took them home, and started to read. On Saturday, I had lunch with my son, Jordan, and I told him what I was doing. He asked me what I was going to write about and I told him East Jerusalem, that fucked up holy land with no dogs. He said, "No, that's not Bukowski." Then I said "George Bush, the anti-Christ," and Jordan said: "No, no politics. Write about Aunt Rachel."

My sister Rachel was the meanest drunk I have ever known. She'd have one sip and turn into hell on earth. One tossed-off remark of hers was: "You know, Sally, I've always wondered if Dad was really your father, I think it might be Uncle Joe." I'm not ready to deal with that bitch now, even on paper.

So I went home and read some more. Read about Bukowski's working and drinking and fucking. His life not quite 180 degrees from mine.

I was in my living room sitting in my favorite brown chair with my legs up and Gracie on my lap. The weather had fogged up and the room was cozy. Since I started reading Bukowski, I couldn't listen to my Baroque music anymore. Marvin was asleep, as usual. The house was quiet, really quiet.

Then I felt it. I felt it coming. A little fart, I could tell it would be small and quiet. Nobody was around. Gracie wouldn't care. She might even like the smell. I let it go. It was quiet all right, but juicy, like there was something there, something in my pants. I knew I had to get up but I had to finish the chapter. He was about to rape a woman. I couldn't quit reading. Eventually, after another page, he did.

I pushed Gracie off my lap and walked stiffly down the hall to the bathroom. Pulled down my pants and I was right. There was something there. I had shit in my pants. It was brown and watery and I thought I had lost at least five pounds. When you're fat you look for any way to lose weight. Carefully, very carefully, I cleaned myself up. Washed myself all over with warm water. It felt good. If you guys don't know, women have to be very careful because of the dreaded bladder infection and who wants to walk around smelling of shit?

I got up, changed my pants and all my clothes. I felt okay. It was just a one-off. I had probably drunk too much Diet Coke over lunch with Jordan. I can't drink that shit. I tightened my asshole and went back to the book. I've got to figure out how that guy could drink so much, eat so much crap and still write like that.

It might take a while.

To Be Fabulous

It was my birthday, which is always a good time to be thinking about death—I love the way burials have gotten green—I think I'll probably want that. One thing I do know is I don't want my kids worrying about what to do with my ashes—I don't want to be in a coffee can lost in someone's garage—dump me in the ocean, or something like that, easy and cheap.

There are so many ways to die—is it better to pay almost 10,000 dollars and die in a sweat lodge in Sedona, in a crash on the freeway, or drop from the sky in a plane with a bunch of strangers.

Is it better to be happy and die?
Is it better to be sad and die?
Is it better to be angry and die?
Is it better to be fat and die?
Is it better to be thin and die?
Is it better to be stupid and die?
Is it better to be smart and die?
Is it better to be awake and die?
Is it better to be asleep and die?

I have decided it is better to be fabulous and die. To be outrageous. To still be alive and die. To have turned over every stone, rock, clump of dirt in my life, every talent, glimmer and good piece of my life, every shining thing that I can think of and then I can laugh, or at least smile.

I shall be the Cheshire Cat of death. When I die, I shall be alive.

The Nectar of the Gods

How dare you? How did you have the nerve, the unmitigated gall, to leave me a note, on a crinkly used piece of cheap paper, to tell me that you're leaving?

You asshole, you squinty-eyed, jug-eared piece of shit, how dare you treat me like this after ten years. Leaving me on a cheap piece of white, blue-lined paper—you corpulent, crepescent, balding excuse for a man—on paper!

You wrote, and I quote—"It's not you, it's me, my fault—I take full responsibility for my actions." How magnanimous, how charitable, how kind! My life is shattered in a million pieces, my self-worth has been flushed down the toilet and it's not my fault! Thanks be to God. And you take full responsibility for it—even better. How comforting, how reassuring, how life-affirming.

I now take full responsibility to tell you that you're a hypocritical excuse for a human being. The fact that you can perambulate on two feet and have a minuscule vocabulary is all that separates you from a jackass.

And knowing that you're leaving me for your baby-doll secretary that you've been screwing behind my back for the past year adds insult to injury. You bobble head, you whining puling prick. Finding happiness, or should I say preying on someone younger than your daughter. For shame.

I keep telling myself that it's not my fault. If it's true, as you say, I'm innocent and you're guilty, then I'll take this opportunity to switch places with you and become guilty so that I can repent. I am accomplishing this feat by raining curses down on your bald pate—many curses, the curses of the doomed.

You had your secret and so did I, my beloved. I never told you this, but while you were shagging your piece of fluff, I was attending meetings—my meditation nights. I regularly met with a group of my sister witches—a full fledged coven and, in an emergency telephonic convocation, we have arranged for a set of curses to be rained down upon you as appropriate punishment for you cowardly, dastardly ways:

1. You will be able to have sex—as much as your craven penis desires. But you will have no pleasure. It has been decreed that the pleasure center in your brain be deleted.

2. You will of course, always be able to ejaculate, except that each

ejaculation will be purple (a color much favored by the Iraqis and squid).

3. Say goodbye to your favorite standards—those old tunes well-beloved by you—Cole Porter, the Gershwins and Irving Berlin. Every piece of music that you hear will be transformed to either heavy metal or hip hop or both, combined. Say hello to JayZ with Linkin Park and Korn. Maybe you can sing those tunes to your beloved.

I write this with sadness and sorrow. I take no joy in your continuing misfortune. As your currently corpulent body withers and becomes flabby and your face falls down to your neck and your last hair falls out. I'll be listening to "That Old Black Magic" and toasting you, my former beloved, inamorato, with the effervescent nectar of the Gods appropriate for someone of your ilk, Diet Coke.

The Silver Bracelet

I'm talking to the old Indian on Lincoln Boulevard.
He sells silver and turquoise jewelry at a stand on the sidewalk.
I love all of the bracelets, but there is one that I like
especially because of the color of the turquoise.
The blue of it reminds me of Easter Eggs.
I say to him, "I really like this one."
He asks me, "Why?"
I say, "Because the turquoise has the color
of a blue Easter egg and I love Easter."
He says, "I'm glad it reminds you of something so nice. It's $8.95."
I say, "I wish I could afford it."

The Indian tells me how his people have been abused.
He tells me of life on the reservation.
I listen, a fourteen-year-old who understands abuse.
A girl who wears Blue Grass toilet water and dreams.

I see him about twice a week
after my tennis lessons in Lincoln Park.
I look at the same bracelet every time and tell him
how much I like it. He says, "It's $8.95."
I say, "I can't afford it."
But he is nice to me and tells me more stories.

I am there at Tex's Tennis Shop and I take lessons in the park.
I take the stairs to the beach and try to swim in the ocean,
coming home with grains of sand,
home to the drunken sister who rages herself to sleep.

All this sun is new to me. My father has a stroke
and my mother has to get rid of me,
and my sister has to take me in with her two damaged boys
and an ill-fitting husband.

I scoff at the brown-green grass and the beige houses.
I laugh at the drive-in and the girls on roller skates.
There is too much sun for me.

I leave, never to return, I think,
and forget everything, except for Tex's Tennis Shop,
and the Indian and the silver bracelet
he gives me when I leave.

The Mockingbird

I saw him again this morning at dawn.
He was on top of my barren birch tree.
Singing his songs, changing them,
performing his best hits to attract his future mate.
Gracie rubbed against my pajama leg,
eager for a treat.

I looked again at the birch tree,
gray branches against the bluing sky.
There were two crows parked beneath.
They weren't tapping their feet, but they were silent.
This time of day, they're usually at a meeting of crows.
I listened until he flew away.

Gracie was sitting at my red door, waiting.

The Touching Pool

It was late January, the dreary time of year. The time of year when I'm broke from Christmas, the time of year when I'm fat from the holiday food and the time of year when I'm just beginning to dread Valentine's Day.

The phone rang, scaring me. It never rings. It was my home phone, not my cell. I let it ring a few times before I picked it up. It was probably someone looking for money.

"Hello," I said.

"Kim, it's Molly from the office."

Molly, Molly—it took me a while to figure out who she was. Oh, yeah, the new girl in the office. I picked up my pen and the message pad and shoved Joey from my lap.

"Hi Molly, what's up?" My voice was hoarse from not speaking to anyone all morning.

"I was wondering if you'd like to go to Vegas this weekend," she said.

I stood up, pulled my blue robe over my pink pajamas and started to pace back and forth in the kitchen, the phone in my hand. Molly—I hardly knew her. Vegas—the answer to my prayers. Money—I had no money. I shut off the radio so I could hear her better.

"Vegas, you said, Las Vegas?"

"Yeah, I got a deal from the Flamingo that's real cheap and I'd like to go with someone. My roommate can't go."

I started circling the kitchen table and turned off the kitchen lights. It would be so good to get away and lie in the warm sun of Vegas and maybe do a little gambling. Getting away, out of town, leaving. My heart was racing. I swallowed to slow my breathing down. She was a gift horse and I had to check it out.

I got all the details. She had even booked a cheap flight. I did have a little money that Mom had given me. I needed this trip.

"What about Joey? I can't afford a kennel, even if I squeak out the money for the trip."

"It's only for two nights, you can probably work something out. My roommate is taking care of Fred and Ginger." Fred, her big mountain dog and Ginger, her cat.

"OK, OK. I'm in. I'll see you at the office. I placed the phone back and ran to take a quick shower and walk Joey so I could get to the office and work out the details.

I am a magician on the phone. I got Bob, my ex, to pick up Joey for the two days. I was sure that he loved Joey more than me. He wouldn't admit it, but he'd be glad to see Joey again. I also went to the bank so I'd have some cash for Vegas. I love to gamble and I hate to lose, I wanted to have my budgeted gambling money ready.

The morning of the trip was overcast and gloomy. I was happy to be getting away and into the desert sun. The phone rang. "Hey Kim, I'm downstairs." Molly was even driving us to the airport.

"Be right down. I can't wait to get out of here."

This early in the morning, on a Saturday, it's easy-breezy to get to the airport. We didn't take the freeway because the 405 is known for mysterious tie-ups at any time, day or night.

We took Southwest, the cheapest and best way to get there. Our seats were OK and the peanuts were fine.

"Molly, I didn't have a chance to thank you for this. It really means a lot."

She didn't reply. I turned to look at her and she was asleep. I wish I could do that. She was sound asleep. I didn't know Molly at all. She was out, all right. She was wearing a baggy dark green sweater, blue jeans and orange crocs. She looked to be in her late thirties, and in this light her skin was kind of pasty looking. I don't like looking at people when they're sleeping. I feel like I'm taking unfair advantage. So I pulled out the airline magazine, full of gadgets that I've never heard of and would never want.

We got in right on time and the landing was smooth. Molly woke up and we got out of the airport and into the taxi line. The weather here was sunny and warm. Perfect. The hotel had our booking and we found our adjoining rooms. The décor of both rooms was orange and green and coordinated with Molly's clothes.

"Molly, what do you want to do? I'd like to try the blackjack tables before it gets too crowded and then go to the pool." I realized that I didn't even know what kind of games she liked to play. "Do you like the slots, or dice? What's your game?"

"Oh I really don't like to gamble. I just wanted to get away. I think I'll get settled in the room, maybe take a little nap. Why don't you call me on your cell when you're at the pool, and I'll join you?"

"OK, I'll see you later." I went down to try my luck. I have this small purse with a zipper that I use at Vegas. I keep my driver's license in it, my credit card, my room keycard and some cash in it so I don't have much to keep track of.

I have a lot of rules about blackjack. I like as small a deck as possible. I hate slow tables. And if I lose to the dealer three times, I move on and if I lose too much, I move out. I also only drink Diet Coke.

I didn't last long. I lost too many times, couldn't' find a good dealer and the tables were all real slow. Also I had to go to the bathroom. Time for the pool.

When I got there, I found two lounge chairs in the shade. I have fair skin and have to be careful of the sun. The pool was full. Full of kids with their pudgy dads and couples, the girls wearing tight bikinis and the men overflowing their trunks. Most of them had skin like mine and were starting to get red from the sun and the beer.

I called Molly, "Hey, come on down. The weather's great and I saved a chair and got a towel for you. Come and meet the folks from Wisconsin. We're in Vegas, baby."

"OK, I'll be down in a few," she said, and hung up.

She came down about a half an hour later. She was wearing a green bikini under her white robe and still had the orange crocs on. Her skin was pale, but not fair, it had a yellowish tinge. She was slim and looked like she never worked out. Her legs were thin and her ankles met each other above her feet, which were large for her body. She took her chair and opened up a book to read.

"Molly, can I get you something?" That's the least I could do. "I really appreciate this trip. Would you like a beer or something now?"

"No thanks, you get something if you want. I'll just stay here. I'll let you know when I'm hungry."

The pool was getting more crowded and the sun was coming out full on, so I thought I'd better take a dip when I can. I'm not much of a swimmer, but I like getting wet.

After a while, I got tired of the Midwestern pool scene and a wet bathing suit and I was hungry. I didn't have time for breakfast and the peanuts were long gone.

"Let's go up, change, and get some lunch," I said to Molly, who was lying in her beach chair with her book across her lap. I couldn't read the title.

"OK, I guess I'm hungry," she said and got herself together and we took the elevator to our rooms.

"I'm starving," I said. "I'm going to take a quick shower, change and I'll knock on your door and we can go eat. Remember, it's my treat."

Fifteen minutes later, I was at her door, knocking. She came right out.

"On the way to the tables, I saw a Mexican restaurant here at the hotel. Is that OK?"

I was hungry and didn't want to start walking around, looking for food.

We took the elevator and found the place. It was dark and cool and half-empty. Perfect. The waitress came, handed us the menus and asked if we wanted anything to drink.

"I'll have a light beer. Molly?"

"A Diet Coke is fine," she said.

"I'm ready for some steak fajitas. All that losing got me hungry. What about you?"

"I don't eat meat. I'm a vegetarian. Sometimes, I'll eat fish. I don't like the idea of an animal being killed for me to eat."

"Yeah. That's the way I am about Bugs Bunny. I'll never eat him or Bambi."

The waitress came and took our order. Molly ordered cheese quesadillas and I went with the fajitas.

"Molly, is everything OK, you seem a little tired. Is it work? Can I help?"

"No, I'm OK. I just need a lot of sleep. Work's fine. You've seen one job, you've seen them all. I'm fine."

"What do you want to do this afternoon? Let's get out of this place and do something different. The weather's good so maybe we could walk somewhere." I can't stand Vegas in the heat.

"Let's take the tram to Mandalay Bay and go to the aquarium. It's small and really neat. I love to look at fish. I love fish," she said.

"OK," I said, "I've never been on the tram. It sounds like fun and it's free, I'm tired of lying around the pool and I hate watching other people gamble. It seems to bring out the worst in them and me."

We walked to the nearest tram stop, which took a while. In Vegas things are always farther than they seem.

We got to the Aquarium. There was a short lineup of the usual suspects from all over the country. It's always Spring Break somewhere. They were dressed in brightly colored resort clothes, like a bunch of parrots. Not the usual L.A. look. The body fat percentage was at the high end. There were a lot of kids. It was a "family attraction."

The Aquarium was low-key, all right. It had huge fish tanks with all sorts of fish. It's called "Shark Reef," emphasizing the big guys. They also had crocodiles and a giant lizard which slept a lot. It took us about forty-five minutes to see the whole thing.

We were at the end of the show and on the way out about thirty feet before the exit there was a large round pool called "The Touching Pool." In it, in about three feet of water, were a variety of baby fish, including one baby shark. We were all grouped around the pool, an even mix of adults and children, leaning over and watching the fish swim by. They kept a perfect circle. At one end was an employee-guide dressed in an outback type suit, looking like Bindy's dad. He had a microphone. He said in a commanding voice: "You can touch the fish, but you can only use one finger, the index finger. Let's see your index finger."

We all dutifully held up the appropriate finger—this was a family event.

"You may not touch the gills or the tail," he continued, "It really upsets them. Remember, only one finger and no gills or tails."

I was watching them swim by and was just getting up my nerve to touch one of them very gently—one that looked the least slimy, when out of the corner of my eye, I saw Molly. The baby shark was directly in front of her and she started touching him right away. I noticed that she was not only touching his back with her index finger, but she was also touching his gills with her other hand.

She let the baby shark go and he swam away. About a quarter of the way around the pool he leaped out of the water. He continued swimming around the circle, however.

When he arrived in front of Molly again she stopped him and started playing with his tail. She was running her fingers around both sides of his tail and seemed engrossed.

All of a sudden there was a loud scream: "TAKE YOUR HANDS OUT OF THE WATER. LEAVE THE POOL IMMEDIATELY!"

I jumped. People had their mouths open and babies started crying. I looked around and everyone was looking at Molly. My God, he was yelling at Molly, the animal lover.

He screamed at her again: "LEAVE THE POOL IMMEDIATELY."

Molly said, "I'm so sorry, can't I stay?"

He said, "NO. How could you be so cruel to an animal? That shark is still disturbed by what you did. It'll take him a while to settle down. LEAVE THE POOL NOW!"

She said, "Please."

He said, "No way. Out."

"Can I look at the other exhibits?" she said.

"Yes," he said. "But get away from the pool now."

Molly put her head down, turned around and slouched towards the exit.

I was still dumbfounded, as were the others. My animal-loving, vegetarian friend, who didn't even eat fish yet had been cruel to one. The guide was still speaking: "That shark is off-limits for touching. He's still traumatized."

I left the area and went looking for Molly. She was sitting on some steps she had found by the entry and tears were streaming down her face. "I'm so sorry. I didn't mean anything. I didn't want to hurt him. I'm so sorry."

I didn't know her well enough to say *what were you thinking?* Or even, why did you do it? I just sat next to her and said inane things like "I'm sure the shark will be okay" and "we can probably come back some other time." But I was shocked and it wasn't okay.

We got on the Tram and walked the long walk back to the Flamingo. Molly was quiet and I continued commenting on things like the weather, people's clothes, traffic, anything I could think of. Molly was silent.

When we got to our rooms I said: "What about dinner tonight? Where do you want to go? Do you want to see if we can catch a show? I didn't spend all of my gambling money."

Molly turned towards me and said, "Kim, you go and do what you want, I've got a headache and I'm not feeling great. I'm just going to take a couple of aspirins and stay in. I'm really tired."

"OK. Whatever you want. But listen, I'll be on my cell and if you change your mind and want to grab a bite or something, just let me know. I'll probably stick around here, the fabulous Flamingo. Call me. I can even bring something up to the room for you, if you like."

She nodded, opened the door I left.

I knocked around the hotel that evening. I tried a little blackjack, but had no taste for it, grabbed a chocolate ice cream cone for dinner and went up to my room. Thank God there was a replay of *When Harry Met Sally* on TV, one of my favorite movies, guaranteed to instill hope in me. No word from Molly. I went to bed.

The phone rang in the morning. Molly said, "Kim, I know our tickets are for 4 P.M., but would you mind if we got an earlier flight? I have a raging headache and I can't get rid of it. I'll even pay the difference, if there's any charge."

I wasn't surprised. "OK, Molly, whatever works for you. Can I bring you anything? Coffee, breakfast, toast, the newspapers, aspirin, anything?"

"No. Thanks for offering. I'm OK. I've had these kinds of headaches before and they just take time to go away. I'll call you if I can get us an earlier flight."

I didn't know what to do. So I knocked around the hotel, had some coffee and toast, went out to the pool fully dressed, sat around and watched people and thought of what I could do if we got home early.

Molly called. "Kim, I got us an earlier flight. We leave at one P.M. I hope that's OK."

"Sure, that's fine. I'm at the pool. I'll come up and we can go to the airport in about an hour. I've been thinking about all of the stuff I can do at home. So that'll be great."

What I was thinking is how I could talk my ex into bringing Joey back early so I could take him for a long walk. The pool was getting crowded with a lot of people with lobster-red skin and I would be glad to get home. Maybe I could talk Bob to coming over for a meal and he'd bring Joey with him.

I left the pool, got my stuff together and knocked on Molly's door. "I'm ready. Let's hit it. I read in the paper that the sun's out in L.A., so that will be a nice welcome for us. How're you feeling?"

"Better, much better. Kim, thanks for understanding. I want to see Fred and Ginger."

"Yeah, I get it. I want to see Joey, too. Unfortunately, he's attached to my ex."

We got in the cab, got to the airport, which was empty for a Sunday afternoon. I tried a few slots. No luck. That's usually when I start winning, when the plane's on the tarmac.

Molly slept on the plane and I reread the gadget book and ate my peanuts. The Diet Coke was flat. I was glad to be going home.

We got to Molly's car and got home with no incident. The traffic was light. We pulled up to my place. Molly got out of the car with me.

"Kim, I'm sorry for messing up this trip for you. It must have been boring. I am really sorry. I wish I'd felt better. I must be coming down with something."

"No. It's OK. It was great to get away and I'm coming home with money in my wallet, so I feel like I'm ahead. Take care of yourself. Kiss Fred and Ginger for me and I'll see you tomorrow.

She took off in her green car and as the car got smaller in the distance I thought that I'll have another shot at seeing the bright lights on the strip in Vegas and I can always think of them like the dreaming spires of Oxford, something to look forward to, something to treasure in my imagination. There's nothing like flying into Vegas at night and seeing those bright lights illuminating the desert. And maybe next time, I'll hit it big.

Ouroboros, or the Snake That Ate Her Tail

Not a cloud in the sky. The wind has died down. I'm at my dining room table as a habanera plays on the radio. Joey's asleep at my side and Gracie's guarding the backyard.

The snake eating her tail is me. The fear in the pit of my stomach travels from there and goes in a circle, around and around feeding on itself.

There's no place else for it to go. No other place to put it. Nothing else that matters. No air, no light, no colors.

Fear arises before thought. My body is engorged with it. My soul is eclipsed with it.

I look for an antidote. Buddha, Jesus Christ, Kwan Yin, Groucho Marx, W.C. Fields, Santa Claus.

Control is an illusion, a myth, something I tell myself I have as I walk down Montana Avenue with a latte in my hand. Especially on a day like this, a day without a cloud in the sky.

This snake is not original to me. It is an ancient symbol called Ouroboros, or "tail-eater." The Egyptians used it as a symbol of the universe—and immortality. The Greeks saw it as "all is one." The Gnostics saw it as the "universal serpent that passes through all things—an unchanging law. And Carl Jung saw the Ouroboros as an archetype and the basic mandala of alchemy—turning lead into gold—a dramatic symbol for the integration and assimilation of the opposite.

So here I am, scared out of my mind, a snake eating her own tail, a snake that slays herself and brings herself back to life.

My Garden

I have a small stone fountain
in the corner of my small garden.
When it's working, it spouts water.
Now, it is quiet.

The sun dapples the page as I write.
I hear the kids playing
and the planes overhead.

In my garden, I am separate, hidden.
I'm sitting inside of an old, gray, weather-beaten fence.
Waiting.

The balls bounce, the birds sing,
The squirrels scamper and I sit and wait.
I sip my Diet Coke from a straw.
It sounds like the can is almost empty.

A bird sings.
It's a mockingbird, full of many songs.
I can't see him.

I also hear an occasional brewer's black bird.
His cry is distinctive.
It sounds like he has a one-note accordion in his throat.

In the distance, a fuchsia-red bougainvillea
climbs on the pale blue garage.

A father coaches his son.

I sit under an old tall pine.
Home to many squirrels, crows
and assorted birds.
It comforts me.

I love sitting here being in everything,
but not a part of anything.
I like sitting outside, being quiet,

being detached, silent under the big tree.
Like Buddha, content with the breezes,
the birds, the kids, the dogs.

Spinning around the sun.

Enlightenment

At 5:02 in the morning of May 25th, 2006
at the Pensione Calcina on the Giodecca Canal
in the Dorsidoro district in Venice, Italy,
I became enlightened.

In an instant I knew who I was before my mother and my father.
I understood the Kabbala, even though I hated math.
I saw Buddha laugh,
Krishna dance,
and Christ heal.

I knew the name of every cat in the world.
I could read and understand *Ulysses*.
Energy really did equal mass times the speed of light squared.
I even understood string theory. Freudian analysis was crystal clear.
I got the collective unconscious and drew a perfect mandala.
Paradise found.

I heard the sound of one hand clapping, I heard the caged bird sing
and the tree fall in the forest.

I was transformed,
in union with the universe.

I was all that I could be.
Gargoyles smiled, pigs flew and the fat lady sang.
Death danced, as the owl and the pussycat sailed down the canal.

My heart overflowed as the hills sang
and the sun was always rising.

That was enough for me.

One Day of Fall

The weather is changing.
We've had our one day of Fall.
I can see the wind moving the trees.
It comes up from the ocean
around four in the afternoon.

The sun is starting to set
making my green garden glow.

Intelligence

Where would I have got if I'd been intelligent?
I mean really smart, Einstein-smart.

I don't fit in my life.
It's becoming narrow
despite TV, the internet and Idol.

I have my appointed rounds and
venture out of the Westside on Thursdays only.

I see the dark-haired gas man who asks the same questions.
The red-headed office manager who knows only one side of me.
I miss the Buddhists. They don't talk.
I sing with one group and write with another.

What could I have been if I'd been smart?
I would be rich, traveling from place to place.
The same places because I'd know what's best.
I would look in the mirror and see a slim well-coiffed woman.
My children would be charming and handsome.
My dining room table would be filled with eloquent guests.

Wait, I'm not writing about intelligence, I'm writing about wealth,
beauty, not brains. I am too stupid to know what smartness brings.

With my luck, I could have married Madoff.

Changes

The weather is turning,
a light chill in the air.
Evening light darkens.
Attention must be paid
or the change will be missed.

Coming home from work today,
I saw a puffy cloud
that bridged the street,
white against the blue sky.

A cloud from childhood
full of dreams.

I was on the street
in a crosswalk,
white stripes on black.
No time for clouds, yet.

Consolation of a Wasteland

"Between the idea and the reality, falls the shadow."
Eliot, T. S. Thomas Stearns, the love of my life,
my teenage life. The life that dreamed of meeting
him on a park bench in Grosvenor Square.
I didn't even know if there was a park bench there.
But that didn't matter. I met him there.

Of course I did most of the talking.
We'd talk of God and the Anglican church and Hopkins,
Gerard Manley, he of the sprung rhythm.

I told him how I hated the Romantics and I didn't care much
for American lit either, except for Mark Twain, who was funny.
I loved Milton and Chaucer. Sabrina Fair and the mind
is its own place, it can make a hell out of heaven or a heaven out of hell.

I loved all those words and the Book of Common Prayer.
Let me be the apple of your eye. There is no health in us.
Agnus Dei, Lamb of God. Have mercy on us.
I want mercy and God and all those words.
I want to chew them, spit them out.
I want to hold them in my mind and go back to them for comfort.

Most of all it's the shadow spaces that I covet.
I have a little shadow that goes in and out with me.
That's when I first learned about shadows.
You can't get rid of them. You can pray all you want, pay money to shrinks,
gurus and holier-than-thou types,
and your shadow will always be with you.

I collect shadows. I know the best shadows in town.
There is even one on my street. I know its comings and goings.
I thought of having a tour of shadows my city,
but who would come with me?
Besides, I don't want to share.
I live in my shadow
There is no room for others.

Lines

"It's snowing down south."
That's what they'd say if my slip was showing.
In the days when we wore slips.

Now they tell me to watch my line lengths.
I never can be neat. Have everything in its place.
Stuff is always leaking out.
Like blood.

The Train

I am on the New York Central speeding out of the city,
through Harlem first, then Yonkers, then Westchester.
The Hudson River Valley. It's beautiful and I am free.
I'm fourteen on my way to college,
out of the house, really out of the house.
Away from grasping minds, hands and voices.
I am deliciously afraid. I am so scared, I can taste it.
The wheels turn and say I'm alone, I'm alone.
I know no one and no one knows me.

I am wearing a gray and white two-piece dress.
I bought it myself at Macy's, I picked it out myself.
I paid for it myself. The skirt is snug
and the top is too big around my shoulders.
That's the way it is. My way. My body.

I see a pretty girl across the way. She's still on the train.
She reads a book and stops to look out the window.
It's getting dark.
She sits on the left side. I always sit on the right.
I'll give it a few hours, and if she's still there, I'll ask her.

May 23, 2010

The Day of Tongues, Pentecost,
the day when everyone could understand everyone else,
the day when red flames of the Holy Spirit
came down and touched everyone,
each one of us, and we all understood,
we all knew what each of us was saying.
Every word, every thought, every idea,
even before it was born.
The word made flesh.
The word, the one true word,
we all knew it.

This morning I woke up dreaming
of a turtle swimming in beautiful
blue clear water, with the sun streaming down
making a path for him.
The water was clear, blue, perfect,
and this turtle, my turtle,
loved it and was happy.

Now the turtle is gone.
I'm scared that he's in the Gulf
or somehow caught in the loop.
I want to be in the loop.
I want to be in the know.
I want to know how.
I want to be known.
I've always wanted to know.
That's all I've wanted.
I want to know
I want to do the right thing.
I want to know what's right.
Who to be.
What's my name?
Where's my Habitat?
What should I be doing?

When in disgrace with fortune and men's eyes.
I know that. I live that.

I don't want to be seen.
I have no lover to turn to.
I beweep too.
Who cares? Who will watch out for me?

Where did the words go?
Why are the eyes so cruel?
I know I'm a little crazy.
Just a little.
There's no meanness in me.
Not that I know of.
Would you tell me if you saw it?
Could you? That's not asking for much.

I don't want much.
I only want to fit in—to be unseen, unborn.
I want to be a fly on the wall.
I am the perfect wallflower.
Don't look at me. Don't touch me.
I do not want to be seen.
Not by you or anyone.
If there is a god out there, or a supreme being,
stay away from me—just pass on by,
Holy Spirit—pass on by and leave me glued,
painted on the wall.
Let me be a flower, a fake one at that.
I do not want to be real.

There is no Holy Spirit.
There is no one. Not one.
The turtle is gone.
Remember the voice of the turtle.
That's from the Bible.
That voice is dead.
No one knows, not a clue.
The red flames are gone.
We sit here alone.
Absent from one.

May 23, 2010

Pretty Girl

I've always wanted to be pretty.
Not gorgeous.
Not beautiful.
Pretty. Passing fair. Nothing excessive.

I've always wanted to fit in.
Be everyone's friend.
Reliable. Compatible. Steadfast.

All the clocks in my house read different times.
I'd like to write that it is my house,
but it's not, it's the bank's.
I'm still paying them for it.
I live in it, me and the dog.

It's a big thing to live in a house alone.
I'm looking at my creeping fig.
Writing on my table.
Generating my own trash.
Separating out the recyclables.

I want to be buried deep in the ground
So that I can be recycled.
A fitting end for the pretty girl.

My Personal Saint

Hair, I've always had a good head of hair.
I notice people's hair.
There is a homeless woman who has a good head of hair.

She walks on Montana Avenue,
my red-headed saint, that I call Teresa
after the Spaniard, not the Albanian.

She is wrapped in Army blankets.
And screams at me in her high-pitched
rusty voice: "Can I have a dollar?"

I obey, as I would any saint.
She likes bills better than coins.
I have yet to find her shrine.
And I've revered her for many years.

She's gotten old. Her hair is turning
from red to gray.
There's competition now.
A black man on 14th St.
He sits. She walks.

I haven't changed. My hair's the same,
fine, thick and blonde.
I have money, so I don't change.
I give out dollars.

When I'm put in the oven,
they'll say, all of them—my priest,
my children, my grandson,
my ex- and current lovers,
the postman, the bank clerk,
my trainer, my chiropractor,
my shrink,
all of them, every single one of them—
they'll all say:
"She had a great head of hair."

Partly Cloudy, Mostly Sunny

My life in four words.
I knew it was going bad in kindergarten
when Mrs. Carat took the ruler
that I was using to conduct "The Star Spangled Banner"
and gave it to a boy who had no sense of rhythm.
I was better, and I knew it.

It was all because of that thing between his legs.
That's what we called it then—"that thing"
He could stick it out from his pants
and hold it between his fingers.

I was set to be a mommy, a stewardess or a nurse.
He would be a dad, a doctor or a pilot.
Even in kindergarten, I could see the fault lines.
No one else did.

So what do you do when you're fine
and you know you're always going to be second best, or third?
Not because of who you are and how you do something,
but because you're a girl and a future Mommy of America.

If you're like me, you don't lose the itch,
the inner eye, the knowing, and you keep doing.
Word after word. Scene after scene.
And you know that there was one true moment
when you nailed that Banner and you liked doing it.
Now you conduct stirring Bach Cantatas in the kitchen.

That smart-ass five-year-old is still there.
In the hospital when they try to bully her,
she looks them in the eye and says: "No."

I need more images. The maroon/gold tablecloth.
The gold/maroon chairs. The lavender Easter Bunny,
who overstayed his welcome.
The sound of the exhaust fan from the second bathroom.

Damn, I'm good. I'm smart, articulate, funny.
I've seen it all, starting with the elevator operator in Bellevue,
who, when a man ran into his elevator
with blood spurting from his neck, said:
"You ain't going to make it, buddy. That's an artery."

Back in New York, sitting in the jam-packed, hot,
muggy subway, rubbing against strangers' bodies,
trying to get to work without being mugged,
I put on the mask when I finally get a seat,
my ears attacked by metal on metal.
The hole that my father lived in for forty years.

I take the good with the bad,
the bad with the good.
Partly cloudy, mostly sunny.

My old dog snores in the chair
and twitches during dreams.
The young one guards the back yard
and my husband brushes his teeth.

When Worlds Collide

I'm having trouble with my mind.
It jumps around and skitters,
looking for disasters and black holes,
things that go bump in the night.

I protect myself with white light,
birds, creeping fig and Gracie, the dog.
sometimes, even people, but I find
they have lost their juice.

I sit here at my desk with the light shining down,
blue pen in my hand, purple yoga mat
rolled up in the corner. The faded yellow
rugs from Turkey on the floor.
And Gracie snoozing on the green overstuffed chair.

I sit here, comforted by small things.

The Street

This afternoon I walked down Montana Avenue
to get a cup of coffee. Nothing fancy,
just a decaf. It was warm and sunny,
a typical February day this year in Santa Monica.

I walked on the north side of the street
past Fred's clothes, past the bank, past the jewelry store.
I stopped at the last window, just for a look.
When I turned around, right in front of me, in front
of my face, two inches away, was the homeless woman,
the one I call St. Theresa, the Spaniard, not the Albanian.

She stopped, looked me in the eye, blocked my path
and asked in her high-pitched squeaky voice,
"Who do you think you are?" She repeated it
in a louder voice, "Who do you think you are?"

I smiled and tried to walk around her. She blocked my path again.
This time she cried, "Who do YOU think you are?"
I said , "I'm the lady who works up the street. You've seen me a lot."
I reached in my purse: "Here's a dollar," I said.

"No money. Not this time," she said. "You've got to tell me
who you are." People were starting to gather around us.
I was dressed in my California casual clothes
and Theresa was wearing her favorite army blankets,
tied with a rope around her waist.

"I'm Sarah," I said. "You know me. I work up the street.
I just want some coffee." More people gathered,
forming a circle around us.
I was getting hot in the sun
and felt sweat running down my legs.

She kept it up. This mad chant, "Who do you think you are?"
I was back in school in front of an angry nun.
"I'm a wife, a mother, a grandma, a lady who sells houses," I said.

Her voice became piercing, strident. She became taller and self assured.
The crowd was two and three feet deep. I could hear questions
like "What's going on? Who is she? Is she a star or a spy?
What's going on? Where's the police or the paparazzi?"
People were pointing their phones at us.

"I live in a house with my husband and two dogs." I said.
"All I want is a cup of coffee.
I listen to music and birds singing
and tivo *American Idol*, I'm just me."

I felt myself getting smaller and smaller. Theresa towered over me.
"No coffee for you," she said. "No more walks on trendy Montana.
No lattes, no cappuccinos, no *Americanos*.
Who do you think you are?"

Then it came to me. I had the answer, the perfect answer,
the one that would stop her, get her out of my face.
I'd tell her who I was. Who I really was. Who I knew I was.

I opened my mouth, the crowd got silent. Traffic stopped.
Everyone focused on me. Cell phones were replaced
by camcorders, the sun came down to hear, birds stopped singing.
I saw the mayor out of the corner of my eye.

Theresa, who now seemed tall as a building, was wearing
black vestments with a golden sash around her waist.
She became silent, waiting for the word from me,
my secret word, the perfect word.

When all of a sudden, within the blink of an eye,
faster than the speed of light, quicker than you can say jack rabbit,
there was a loud boom and I turned into a huge green and gold
snake-like being, who was very light on her feet.

I opened my mouth, gobbled Theresa up in one big bite,
tiptoed through the tulips, tripped the light fantastic
and shuffled off to Buffalo.

That's who I was. That's who I really was.
That's who I knew I was.

As Paul wrote in First Corinthians:
"For the Kingdom of God
is not a matter of talk
but of power."

The Old Black and White Dog

I know little about moonbeams and marigolds.
That is not the way my life spiraled out.
My quintessential focus has been on animals,
dogs and cats named Jezebel, Arundel, Humphrey and Max
and the black and white dog named Oliver,
who's been my friend these past few years.
Orangutans and chimpanzees have their attractions
as do lions and marmosets, but the black and white dog
has my heart.

The melanoma cracked open my life like a broken porcelain statue,
changing the ecosystem of my life, my tranquility.
Melanoma, a beautiful sounding word like melody.
It's not beautiful, it's treacherous.
It comes from blackness, not beauty.

Cretinous old bats wallow around my lair disturbing
the ecosystem of my tranquility.

It's a question of time, which we all know is of the essence.
Or is it a question of spirit, of souls, of cells?
Organisms lacking essential protective devices fixate
on impenetrable ideas, which continue to malfunction
and erupt in dizzying valences.

Or is it nothing, niente, nada, no thing.
Not here, not there—emptiness devoid.
A void, a caldera.
Empty reflections of former glory.
Vestigial.

Globules of ideas proceed out of nowhere. Cartoonist's bubbles.
Lies, half-truths, wishes, dreams, nightmares.
Snow White becomes the Cat Woman.

We live in an asteroid named Palestrina.
Dancing around the sky in shattered pieces
of forgotten dreams. Idylls not of the king,
but of the plebe. Workers in the land of daily life.

traveling between fixed places, ruled by an unseen,
uncaring sky. The seven sisters of the Pleiades,
not eight as even the fool knows.
They come to us only in our dreams.

Continuing this rush of life, meeting, jarring.
Twisted, bruising, cell upon cell,
rushing towards certain destruction,
oblivious of the consequences.

Identity is lost. Free will absent.
All important is the exuberant mad dash
of cells morphing into each other,
creating patterns previously unseen by the human eye.

The time for dreaming is lost.
No need for future plans.
Each breath is enough.
It's up to the old black and white dog, sleeping in the sun.

I would be happy dying with that dog.

The Frozen Child

There are people I've hurt.
I wear my regret like a wound on my body.
Each line represents a wrong turn,
a lie, a missed opportunity,
a botched action, a missing person.

I still grieve over my biggest regret,
not being nice to my favorite uncle
the day of his death when I was nine.
I loved him so much and I was mean to him.

I'll always bear that scar.
I can't get past it.
My every action is related to that Saturday.

I was his vanilla girl. His princess.
He was my teddy bear.
Uncle Joe, my protector, my guardian angel, my intercessor.

I'm in my own home.
My yellow purse is on the dining room table.
The pen with cobalt ink is in my hand.
My dog goes into the backyard to find new smells.
I sit here, looking old and substantial.
But I'm really that little girl, back in Goshen,
whose uncle just died.
Who can't see colors anymore, who can't taste food,
who can't stop crying.
Don't make me kiss him.
I can't look at that body in the living room.

I surround myself with barking dogs and baroque music.
My hand keeps working.
I loved a dying man and keep him alive by remembering.

THEN

*It's better to travel well
than to arrive.*

Buddha

When I Was Small

When I was small everyone was so big.
They walked around and didn't see me.
I could see them from beneath
the table, but they couldn't see me.

When they did see me,
I was either crying or scared.
"She's too sensitive.
I've never seen a child like that.
Rachel, you spoil her."

I held on to a dog or cat or Uncle Joe
and the bigs kept on talking.
"She's too nervous. She ought to eat more."

My mother made me spell for them.
I was a genius at spelling "insurance,"
the same word over and over.
The big people loved it
and the little ones didn't care.

The bigs had no idea how big
they were, or when they lifted me,
how high they'd carried me.
Their voices were loud and emphatic
like squawking parrots.

Now I am big
and the small part of me is still there,
especially in elevators or crowded rooms.
I back up against walls for protection
and check shadows, even in daylight.
My dog is my keeper at night.

The Sea Monsters

The sea monsters came to me
in a dream last night.
They were slippery and slimy
and oozed with a sticky substance
that clung to my skin and smelled of death.

They wanted me to dance,
to play with them in the sea.
They said I was one of them,
as they wrapped their tentacles
around my legs.

They said it wouldn't hurt,
as they slimed me with their seed.
Their colors were dark. Gray and green
and brown, and their smells—
their smells were of dead rats
oozing slime like seaweed.
I stepped on something gelatinous.

I try to get free and become
more entangled.
My hair falls in my eyes
and I can't tell
where the monsters end
and the seaweed begins.
I'm cold and it's now dark.
I can't see.
I can feel their slippery touch
writhing up and down my legs.
I am a prisoner.

Jimmy calls: "Sally come and play."
We're at the house in the country,
in Goshen—the land of milk and honey,
The home of Uncle Joe and Buster, the dog.

"Is Mommy back?"
"No, come and play with us,"
my older brother calls.
"I've got something to show you."

He's in the living room
With his friends and he has his pants
open, with his thing in his hand.
He says: "Here's my banana
Put it in your mouth and taste it.
See, it's just a banana."

I know it's wrong
and I don't want it,
but he's my brother
and I love him and Mommy's gone.
The boys are laughing
and he's following me
with it hanging out of his pants.
"It's a banana, come on."

The monsters come back.
Now they're big and strong
and don't need water anymore.

I get up and walk into
my pink bathroom with the picture
of the bunny rabbit on the wall
and the orange flowers in the blue pot.
I stick my head over the white toilet
and I puke green vomit,
the spittle running down my cheek.

I can hear the monsters.
I can hear Jimmy and the boys.
I turn my head to face them,
and they're gone.

I know better. They're here
within me, even now.
Even in this room with

the red tablecloth
and the green birch trees outside.

Even in this room with
the music on the radio. I can open
my mouth and they will fall out.
My pen cannot control them.

Those laughing boys and the slimy sea monsters haven't left me.

Don't Tell

She bought me a pair of shoes,
crappy brown shoes.
the bribe, the fucking bribe,
for what I saw.

I was eleven. I came home
early from school that day.
Not too early,
only twenty minutes or so.

The door was locked.
It's never locked.
I rang the bell and pounded
and pounded and yelled for my mom.

Then she came out, all messed up
in wrinkled clothes
"You're home early," she said,
and she let me in.
I saw him running down the stairs
of our upside down house.

I went into the living room
and saw the pillows crushed
at the end of the couch.

Nothing. Nothing.

I knew. At eleven, I knew.
I heard him sneaking out.
The door slammed behind him.
She begged, pleaded,
don't tell Dad, don't tell.
He'll kill me. He'll kill Mr. Rauch.
I hated that name.

He'll kill me. Don't tell.

What a dumb fucking cunt
my mother. The one who
pushed me to go to Sunday School.
She had a picture of Jesus over her bed.

I didn't tell.

It lasted until I was thirteen.
I failed at school,
gained twenty pounds.
I had to sit around while guarding the house.
I had to eat.

I didn't tell.

I ate every sweet thing.
Twinkies, Peanut Butter Cups,
Milk Duds, Malomars,
Anything I wanted
as I watched the house.

She couldn't stand it any longer.
We all moved to the country
(except Mr. Rauch)
to escape the big city
but I didn't tell. I never told.

Aunt Sis

She was a woman enveloped by darkness. Not the magical kind, but the darkness of sheer dirt and grime. She was short and lumpy, like a filthy doughboy.

I remember that she had dark, stringy hair that she knotted in a careless bun. Her clothes were sloppy and mismatched and I can even remember that her stockings were droopy and always had runs. She wore black, low-heeled shoes that laced up.

I don't remember much about her face, except that she had a mole on her chin with a long black hair growing out of it. She terrified me. Her voice was cracked and loud. It penetrated my bones.

The last time I saw her was when I was seven years old. She and my Uncle Paul had an apartment in the Bronx. She was my mother's sister, hence the "Aunt Sis." I tried to get out of going, but it was a family duty.

Uncle Paul was quiet and gentle. We used to trade comics. I'd give him my *Looney Tunes* and *Wonder Woman* and he'd give me *Superman* and *Captain Marvel*.

I had never been to their apartment before. We walked up the stairs of the stone gray apartment building. They had to buzz us in. I remember the smell of paint and the look of the green-flaked stripe on the wall.

We were at her door and my father rang the bell which didn't work. He knocked. Someone came to the door and opened it. It was my Aunt Sis, she was so dark and the place was so black, I could only see her silhouette.

The smell of that moment, it attacked my nose like a rat, like everything I'd ever been afraid of in my life. It smelled of death, decay, garbage and things not even mentioned in fairy tales.

I refused to enter. My mother dragged me in and there I was in Aunt Sis's lair. My Uncle Paul wasn't home. She offered us tea and cake on chipped cups. I refused to eat. I couldn't breathe through my nose. I feared the filth would cling to me. I stood behind my father for safety.

I don't know how long I was there. Finally my father took pity on me and we waited outside for my mother. I sucked in the air and the sunshine and checked my body for darkness.

To this day, I don't know the story of Aunt Sis. My mother swore that she was pretty when young and I can vaguely remember seeing a picture of her at my parent's wedding. She had two children, one nice and normal called "Smiles" and one weirdo named Jerry who, according to my mother, was never the same after he dove into an empty pool.

Jesus Loves Me

Jesus loves me.
He does. He really does.
They told me so.

I lie here in my narrow bed
in the upside-down house with thin walls
and I hear them: "No, John no. It hurts."
I hear the pounding noise and it hurts.

I hear it and I hear them
and Jesus loves me.
I don't cry.
I don't say stop.
I don't.

Somehow, I know it's bad and I'm bad
and I can't speak the evil
Jesus loves me, this I know.

And it goes on night after night.

When they put me in bed
my legs start shaking. They shake so much
I can't stop and my teeth chatter.
I shake all over.
Jesus loves me.

What's wrong with you Sally?
What's wrong with her John?
I don't tell because it's bad.
I can't speak. The devil will get me.
I know Jesus loves me.

The doctor came and he jams a wooden
stick in my throat and hammers my legs.
He says, "She'll be fine. She's a little high strung.
Just give her some of this medicine."
Jesus loves me.
The devil came to me in a dream. He ties me up

and says, "Sally tell a lie. Lie for me. Tell a lie."
I fight him. He's a gangster. A thief.
I won't lie. I pray for the bad man.
Jesus loves me.

I go into their room and open the bureau drawer.
I see a jar of yellow, gooey Vaseline
and a package of weird looking rubber things called Ramses.
I know they're dirty and I can't talk about them.

My legs keep shaking.
My father prays over me.
Night after night.
I hear it might be St. Vitus' Dance.
I see myself twitching all over
like the girl on Tremont Avenue.
Why does a saint do that to little girls?
Jesus loves me.

It goes on. I shake.
Daddy prays. Mommy hollers.

I always want the blue and white dish
with the picture of the pagoda on it.
I smear my yellow eggs over it.
I dream I'm a Chinese princess
living there with my panda.
There are no walls, no screaming.
Just me and panda.

The summer comes.
They send me away.
It's too hot in the city.

I sleep.

Jesus loves me.

This I know.

The Surprise

It was a great day. A perfect day. My birthday day. My fifth. My birthday always came at the best time of the year, in October. The leaves are turning, the air is clear, the sun is warm with just a hint of the cold to come, full of crisp promise and apples.

We were in Goshen, the land of milk and honey, at my Uncle Joe's house. I loved him and his house, his garden and the town, and I really loved being in the country.

Mom had baked a birthday cake, vanilla, because I was the vanilla girl back then and she let me lick the batter spoon and the bowl. That morning Uncle Joe took me into town in Lizzie, his Model T. It was Saturday and all the farmers were there. I played with some of the kids while their folks shopped and I even got an ice cream cone—vanilla, of course.

Daddy had come up from the city and was taking a long nap in the upstairs bedroom.

Uncle Joe was my hero. He was big and round like Santa Claus and I knew he really loved me. One Christmas, early in the morning, I heard some noise on the roof. Someone was walking on it. Then I heard, "Ho, Ho, Ho." Someone was walking down the hall, coming towards my room. I squeezed my eyes shut and hid under the covers, my whole body tingling with excitement. I heard the door open. "Is there a little girl here? I hope she's been good."

I peeked out from under the covers and saw Santa in a red and white outfit, just like in the poem. He had a bag full of toys in his hand. I sat right up and said, "Here I am Santa and I've been very, very good." I knew it was Uncle Joe, my very own Santa. He gave me Andy Panda that year.

He was my best friend and he took care of me when things got tough between Mom and Dad. I remember how he smelled, a combination of Old Spice, the foundry where he worked and his garden, his victory garden.

We had the party in the front room, or as we called it then, the parlor. We never used that room. It was a sacred space for visitors only. The upright piano was there and a couch and two stiff chairs covered with lace doilies that Mrs. Sims had crocheted.

It wasn't a big party. Sonny from across the street came. He had a pony named Billy who was really nasty. The Mayors from next door came and Farmer Jones and his wife and the baby came, too. We really did know a

Farmer Jones. He let me ride his tractor once and we used to get our eggs and milk from him. There weren't a lot of kids at the party because in the country we had to be driven everywhere.

Mom served the cake and ice cream and homemade lemonade with ice that Uncle Joe and I had gotten in town. Since we were in the parlor, which had four windows, two looking out on the porch and two looking onto the side driveway, we could see and hear people coming.

I don't remember all of the presents, but I do remember my favorite one—a pair of majorette boots with white tassels that Uncle Joe had given me. I loved those boots. I strutted around the house with them on, marching and twirling an imaginary baton. There were also dolls and the usual cowgirl pajamas from Aunt Gus.

We heard a truck crunching up the driveway. Mom went to see who it was and it was my cousin Jerry. He was a lot older than me. I hardly knew him. He was tall and had red curly hair and pale skin. The hair on his arms matched the hair on his head."I came to bring Sally a present, he said, "a special one that I got just for her." I was so excited, I couldn't wait.

But Mom made me wait and she gave him his cake and ice cream and lemonade, which took forever. Finally, he said, "Well, I guess it's time. I'll go out and get it."

When he came back from his truck, he had a Velveeta cheese box in his hand. That's the way cheese used to come, in wooden boxes. You'd slide out the top and there'd be the cheese all ready to make a grilled cheese sandwich to go with Sunday night supper tomato soup.

Now, I like cheese as much as anybody, but I wondered what in that box could be so special.

He came up to me and said, "Here it is—Happy Birthday."

I took the box in my hands and slid out the top easily because I knew how to do that, and then everything stopped. In the box, wriggling around, was a black snake, a live snake in that wooden cheese box.

I screamed. Uncle Joe grabbed the box out of my hand and looked in. Everybody looked at me while I screamed and cried, "Don't hurt the snake. Put it back in a field far from here. But don't kill it." I knew country people killed a lot of snakes. I don't know what happened next. I do know that it took Uncle Joe a long time to calm me down. Cousin Jerry, the snake, and his truck were soon gone.

Dad said, "You know, Sally, it was only a harmless garter snake," but I didn't care.

"Cousin Jerry hasn't been the same since he dove into that empty pool," Mom said.

I only saw Jerry a few times after that: at his wedding, when he married Florence, and when they baptized their baby girl, Sandy. Then they moved up to Maine. He left the house for work one day and never came back.

Mother Love

I knew my mother loved me
because she told me so.
Like Jesus, she told me.
Jesus loved me, the Bible told me so.
So did my mother.

I knew she loved me because
she dressed me every day.
And made me eat food that I hated
because it was good for me.
I had to eat for all the starving children in China,
who were exactly on the other side of the world.
I wished there was a hole that would send me straight through.

She loved me because she did my homework
and we went downtown every year in August
to get the special edition of the textbooks,
the ones with the answers in the back.

She loved me. She pushed me.
She lied for me, and to me.
She forged school papers to have me skip a grade.
She hovered. She was always there from "sleep tight,
don't let the bedbugs bite" to "rise and shine."

Now, I know that on the day when I came home from school
and found her fucking Mr. Rauch, Dad's best friend,
she let me catch her out of love for me.
She knew that we had to break up.
I was eleven, soon to be in high school.
It was time for me to go.

The second time I discovered her with Mr. Rauch was the summer
    I was twelve.
I came home early from a movie because the projector broke.
I was walking down the wooden steps to the house
when I saw him shutting the front door on his way out.
He put his head down and ran up the steps.

She put me in her story.
I didn't want to be in her story.
I had no choice.
She put me in it.
It was time for me to go.

Now, all these years later,
I realize this as I look back.
Her gift of letting me find her twice freed me from her grasp.
It got me out of the Bronx, and away from her.

So Mom, like Jesus, you did love me. I know it.
You made me stand on my own.
Kicked me out of the nest like the fledgling that I was.
If it weren't for you, I wouldn't be here now listening to Mozart
hearing my husband turn the pages as he reads the Sunday paper.

Rachel

My older sister Rachel
came to me in a dream last night.
She was young and beautiful
with dark movie-star hair,
deep blue eyes and a gleaming smile.

She was not the bitch she-goddess of my youth.
The one who turned mean on a dime
and slew me with words like "Your ears
really stick out" and "Your hair looks
like the wild woman of Borneo."

Rachel sent me on many errands.
One time I was turned away
by Mrs. Marconi at the corner store.
When I showed her the note from Rachel,
Mrs. M. said, "Sanitary napkins?
You tell your big sister to get them herself."

Rachel used to babysit me
and pay me to leave the house
when her boyfriends came over.
She taught piano on Saturday mornings
in our living room and I wasn't
able to listen to *Let's Pretend*
on the radio because of the noise.

One cold, winter morning Mom, Rachel
and I were in the kitchen. I was reading
Wonder Woman comics and eating cereal
when all of a sudden the room got quiet.
The air was sucked out.
I heard the word "late."
Mom jumped up to get to the wall calendar.
I didn't know what was going on.
I kept my head down so they wouldn't
kick me out of the kitchen. I didn't want
them to notice me.

I needn't have bothered.
They didn't pay any attention to me or anyone else.
I had a great week of freedom from them both.
I kept my head down and kept quiet.
I could breathe in my own home at last.

The House of Secrets

My father, the big red giant,
never heard anything.
Secrets buzzed around him like drunken wasps.
He went to work wearing his engineer's cap
and carrying a lunch pail. Came home,
wrapped himself in a brown Army blanket,
sat on a grey chair in the living room
and prayed.

My house was the house of secrets.
Thick secrets, like banners hanging
from the piano. Dumped across the kitchen table.
Displayed in front of our house
Like a gold-star mother's flag.

If you listened you could hear them.
They came over our Stromberg Carlson radio
through the static when my father tried to tune it.
You could hear them in the crack of my mother's
voice when she tried to sing.
If you'd bother to ask my cat, Tiger,
or my dog, Jeep, they'd tell you
because they knew everything.

One day Rachel, my older sister, left the house early
to go to Jersey City for a school project, she said.
She came home late in the day, all doubled over.
She went to bed with the flu
and skipped school for days.
It soured me on Jersey City.

She married her boyfriend and had us over for holiday meals.
She got drunk and passed out in bed every time.
One drink and she became an assassin.
She needed no weapons, only her words.
We were silent, participating in our own murders.

I left the house as soon as I could.
Leaving the house, the animals and the secrets.

I left and didn't look back afraid of the banners of secrets
and afraid of becoming like Rachel, my big sister,
who watched out for me when she could.
I knew what was best for me, to get away
as far and as fast as I was able and I've never stopped leaving.

But last night, in my dream, Rachel was beautiful.
I told her she was welcome in my dreams at any time.
We could go to Jones Beach and lie on the warm sand
and look at the waves crashing on the shore.
We could bring a portable radio, Ritz crackers, peanut butter
and cokes listen to Frank and Bing,
and argue about who was prettier, Rita Hayworth or Ava Gardner.

Sonny

In the country, we used to go on long walks on dirt roads, going nowhere.
We'd pack a picnic and just take off.

My friend Sonny and I would take our two dogs, Buster and Pal.
We used to go to a place we called the jungle.
There were vines hanging from trees we could swing on like
Tarzan and Jane.

We walked and walked. I was usually barefoot
and could feel the dry dust between my toes.
We looked for shade when we got hot.
Sonny scouted for snakes and I told stories from my favorite fairy tales.

Sonny loved to show off.
One time he showed me his penis and how he could pee standing up.
He said he was better than me. I didn't care.
In the country, cows and horses can pee standing up.

He said he didn't know where his mother was
and I told him my father was in the city.
We carped about school, teachers and the school bus driver.
When we ate, the food was great.
Velveeta cheese on white bread wrapped in wax paper.

We walked and walked. Sonny and I.
Nothing between us in a jungle populated
by bugs, birds and a few harmless snakes.
We crossed over brooks and creeks and rickety bridges.
We heard trains in the distance and open and closed farmer's gates.
We never got lost.

Nothing remains.
I walk different paths now.
There's not much grass and just a few birds and trees.
I'd like to go back there and walk with Sonny and the dogs
and tell him what a good guide he was
and that I'd learn to pee standing up, if I have to.

The Cold Pool

On a hot summer's day in August
we walked to the cold pool at the top of the hill.
I was barefoot, as usual, and felt
the sting of sharp grass and small stones on my feet.

We talked of who was better, Wonder Woman or Superman.
I knew that Wonder Woman ruled and sometimes Sonny agreed.
It was hot and the sun beat down on my back.
The sky was bright with no clouds.

When we got to the pool, no one else was there.
We were glad because it belonged to the Hotel.
We spread our towels on the warm cement
and went in, feet first, feeling the cold rush up into our bones.

Sonny, my best friend, the boy across the street,
the boy who could do anything, milk cows, catch frogs,
climb trees, herd chickens, and swing from vines like Tarzan.
We swore to stick together and we vowed it in blood.

Scavenger

I scour my memory for the past.
I have no present.

Walking, that's what I remember.
Walking barefoot on a dusty road.
The feel of the loose dirt between my toes
and the sharp pain of an unseen stone.

Barefoot was my way.
Nothing between me and the dirt.
Shoes were for the city.
In the spring, squeezing mud between my toes.

Sonny Jones lived across the street.
He was a brash country boy
who loved to show me how he could pee standing up.
He could pee anywhere.

We went on jungle walks. Exploring.
We never found an elephant or tiger.
Just some quiet cows mulching their cud.
The occasional bull was memorable.

We crossed ditches, creeks, no rivers.
we climbed hills, no mountains.
When we saw a snake, Sonny would pick it up
and tease me with it.
I could never get over being afraid.

We walked and walked and walked,
talking of Tarzan, Cheetah, Superman and the Green Hornet.
We'd come home dead tired.

We vowed always, always, always
to be friends and exchanged blood vows
from pricked fingers.

But no, I went away to school.
I am always leaving people.
I left them all, every single one.
I never looked back.

Until now.

Old Tom

In Stockbridge there
was a man we all called "Old Tom."
He had a horse and buggy
and would come to meet
each train, every day.

He dressed in army blankets
and sat up tall, holding his whip
and never using it.
He would proceed in a stately manner
up and down Main Street
to and from the train station.

I asked who he was and why does
he go there all the time.
Who is he meeting?
Nobody knew. Nobody cared.
Some said he used to deliver
the mail before we had cars.
Some said he was waiting for someone
who never came.

Old Tom didn't talk.
Didn't stop for a chat.
Just went up and down Main Street,
his eyes straight ahead.
There was room for someone
like that in the town,
someone who knew his job.

Uncle Dick

Uncle Dick was a slight man
with bright blue eyes.
He talked with a pipe clenched between his teeth
and said "aayeh" for yes in that Yankee way.

He was a caretaker and fixer of other people's homes
and gardens and hopes and dreams.
He would take me on walks and show me
what he did for summer people.
He could pick berries faster than anyone,
Uncle Dick could.

He didn't talk much.
He left the talking to the aunts.
He ate cornflakes, milk and a banana every morning.
He did chores, drove my aunt back and forth to work
to the post office every day. He shoveled snow.
Knew the best fishing in the county.
Smoked his pipe and said "aayeh."

He was good to be with, Uncle Dick.
Never asked any questions.
Was always ready with a small smile.
Kept his garden in good order.
Prepared houses for winter and summer.
Took a nap every day and one day,
well into his eighties, he didn't wake up.

Uncle Lloyd

Uncle Lloyd came to me in a dream last night and was very kind to my son. This was also true in real life. He gave him a signed Dodger ball.

Uncle Lloyd was a Christmas uncle. One unknown to me. We would sit around opening presents on Christmas Eve and there was always one from Uncle Lloyd all the way from California. Every year the same present, dried fruit wrapped in yellow cellophane in a flat straw basket. Why couldn't it have been chocolate?

On Christmas day there was the ritual of the phone call either from or to California. Always through the long distance operator. Sometimes it would take hours to get through, but the aunts never gave up. We would all stand around the phone waiting for our turn to speak. I never knew what to say to him or he to me, though the aunts insisted I talk.

He was the golden boy, the baby who had made something out of his life. He had become an officer in the Army during World War II, a lieutenant or a captain. He attended college, the first in our family. He never graduated but ended up with a good job at the Pickwick Bookstore in Hollywood, the aunts thought he might have been the manager. And he had a friend, maybe a girlfriend, the aunts always hoped, who was a famous hairdresser to the stars—Joann St. Oegger. Every movie that we saw we would dutifully look for her name in the credits and very occasionally be rewarded. The aunts lived for that moment.

I met him the summer I was fourteen. The summer I got to live in Santa Monica Canyon with my sister and brother-in-law. The summer I met my first Native American who had a booth on Lincoln Blvd. near Tex's Tennis Shop. He told me the truth about the Indians.

Uncle Lloyd invited us all over to his apartment in Hollywood for dinner. He was medium height with a barrel chest and wore his dark blonde hair in a crew cut. I noticed that his nose got redder as the evening wore on. He always wore, on the third finger of his left hand, a chunky gold ring with a big diamond in the middle. I loved his place. It had dark floors, high ceilings, colorful rugs and lots of books. He served us an elegant dessert of fresh peaches and Roquefort cheese.

Later he took us to the Hollywood Bowl and I heard Cesar Franck's *Symphony in D Minor* for the first time.

The only thing I can remember him saying that night was that he had no idea where my sister and I came from. "How," he said "could Rachel and John have fathered you two. Where did you come from?"

I didn't see him again for many years until my first husband and I moved out to Newport Beach and invited him over for Thanksgiving and Christmas. He'd come about once a year. He had some annoying habits—listening to a football game on his portable radio with earphone, or later watching it on TV, drinking too much and asking that same question over and over—where did my sister and I come from.

Around that same time I remember an elegant black and white full-page picture of him that appeared in a Palm Springs magazine. He hit the social scene really hard.

The last time I saw him was the year I divorced. He was my only family aside from my mother and two kids. He came for Thanksgiving to my small rented house in Glendale. I was so grateful to see him; he could have had all the liquor in my house and watched football all day long.

One day, a few years later, I got a call from some attorney. Uncle Lloyd had died alone in his apartment and I had been named the executrix of his will. I had to sort everything out. His current apartment was a dreary flat in Hollywood. The only remarkable thing about it was that he had managed to keep his books. He had become an alcoholic during his last years. I had to open up his safe deposit box, which was empty. He had very little money. The only thing of value was his gold and diamond ring, which he left to my niece. The ring had disappeared. I had only enough money to send his body back to Stockbridge where the two aunts who outlived him awaited.

I thought he might have pawned or sold that ring or that it might have been removed after his death. My sister thought I stole it.

Witness

Now, I am not that close
to earth and nature.

I am in translated nature.
I haven't seen a bird's nest
or a cow pie in years.

But I do remember the time
on Fletcher Avenue
when I almost stepped on a snake
sunning himself in the road.

I was walking on the left side, facing traffic.
The rule that was drummed into me
as a kid in the country.
Nobody told the snake.

I remember stepping on a lot
of warm, brown, smelly cow shit,
cow pies we called them.
And I remember Billy, the pony,
who ran away with me on his back.
I had to fall off
to get off.

The snake and Billy and the cow pies.
They're all mine.

I remember green grasshoppers
and daddy longlegs.
Yellow buttercups.
You could stick your nose in them
and make your nose yellow.
And I remember lightning bugs
flying around in a jar with holes in the top,
lighting my room at night.

They're all a part of me.
I eat them like a warm hunk of bread
and I can only find them in my dreams.
I miss them as if I just turned a corner.
and they've just left.

I know how an outhouse smells.
I know what a Monkey Ward catalogue
looks like with pictures of little girl cowgirls,
and stewardesses and nurses.
Filled with things that we could never buy.

I know about sitting around the kitchen table
by the wood stove, getting warm,
listening to the noon news,
counting the car crashes in winter
and the drownings in summer
and having another glass of lemonade.

The country was not all pretty:
my father bringing home dead rabbits,
my mother plucking feathers from dead chickens,
my brother's favorite Rhode Island Red rooster
flattened by the Model T.

All of this is mine, not yours.
Not one of you has seen or smelled these things.
They're mine, not yours.
I know things.
I know.

Sarah

I haven't written of my namesake,
Grandma Sarah, my mother's mother.
I've heard stories of her all my life.

She was strong.
She was tough.
She hit my brother with a cane for misspelling.
She was fierce with life.

She came over on a boat
during the potato famine.
Landed in New York City
and stayed there.
She married and had five children.

She was a nurse and worked
for doctors in the neighborhood.
Her husband became a drunk and ended up in a cage on Riker's Island.
One of her children worked on towboats in the Hudson
and was murdered with a knife.
Another died of sepsis from a failed abortion.

She was a strong woman, my grandma Sarah.
She took on all comers, including my father.
She was dead before I was born.
I never knew her.
Her shadow stretched out for a long time
and pervaded our house
with the smell of strong soap
and boiled potatoes.

Grandma

One of my grandmothers came to me
in a dream last night.
The one from Stockbridge.
The one whose picture
was in Aunt Gus' dining room.
The one with a big face and piggy eyes.
Eyes that followed me around the room like Jesus.
I never sat with my back to that picture.

She came to me seeping out from a corner,
slipping out from under the bed. She came to me.
She told me of life in Sweden. How cold
and hard it was coming over on the boat with her sister.
Seeking a new life and work in service.

Arriving in New York City, a dirty, scary place,
full of noise. "I was so sick;" she said, "I couldn't stand for three days.
I was so terrified. I wanted to go home.
I met Bernard from Holland. He took me to Stockbridge.

"I loved that town. I loved the smell of the dirt.
The summers, the streets, the trees. The quiet.
We had our own home
I had five children. I worked hard doing laundry.
Heating the water on the wood stove.
Getting everything clean.
The children hanging up the clothes.
And the ironing, always the ironing in the frost
of winter and the heat of summer. Always the hot stove.

"Bernard was a gardener, a good one.
He started drinking and couldn't stop.
He was an angry, bitter man.
The air around him was poison.

"I did it. I worked. I cared for. I scrubbed.
I did it in the small house on Poorhouse Row.
I did it. I named them all. William, John,
Augusta, Teitia, Alice and Lloyd, the baby.
I cleaned. I cooked. I cared."

"Grandma, I see you now. There is no judgment.
No regrets. Only pride. Only two hands
and two feet. My eyes were small in the picture
because of the bright light.
I was not angry, only scared."

"We are part of each other," she said, "you and me.
Now and then and then and then.
We know, don't we? We know what life is.
Look at your feet."

The Mark

I'm not good at keeping things:
Pictures, mementos, keepsakes.
But I do have Grandma's bowl.
I put it in the breakfront in the dining room.
A white porcelain bowl, ornate,
with gold stems and purple flowers circling the sides.
There's an indistinguishable mark on the bottom.
I can't tell if it's a letter of the alphabet,
a number, or a design.
Hardly a holiday goes by that I don't turn it over
and look at it. My only family heirloom.

It was my mother's mother's bowl.
And my mother, Rachel,
who was bad at keeping things,
kept this bowl.
Now I have it.

It's nothing to look at, doesn't fit in my house.
But it is an heirloom,
if an heirloom can be without value.

I will give it to my daughter.
Maybe she'll keep it, or not.
Maybe she'll give it to her daughter, or not.
It has never been broken,
not like my sister and myself,
with indecipherable marks of our own.

Advice

My mother was knocking around in my head last night.
Sally do this, be that, don't tell your father.
If you can't be good, be careful.
Don't tell. Keep quiet. Please don't tell.
Her tears spilled down her face.

She doesn't quit, my mother, doesn't give way.
Your face is your fortune.
Don't put shoes on the table or there'll be a fight.
Say the 23rd Psalm every day before you leave the house.
Be quiet. Practice. Do what they say.
He'll kill me if you tell. Be quiet.

I love you. You're my best girl.
Everything I've done, I've done for you.

You're the smart one.

The Frozen Child

I'll always bear the scar.
I can't get past it.
My every action is related to that Saturday.

It was a summer day in August.
The special kind of summer day,
nothing much going on,
just the warm sun, the chickens scrambling for their food.
Buster, the dog was lying on the cement steps leading to the cellar.
I was barefoot and giving Buster a head rub.

Uncle Joe came out of the garage and said,
"Sally, how about a movie this afternoon?
There's a good one with Wallace Beery playing in town."
I jumped up and said, "Yes, yes, let's go. Can I have some Jujubes?
And I want to pet Lassie." The movie cashier had a collie,
who looked just like Lassie and he was always there beside her booth

We rode in to town in Uncle Joe's Model T.
He wouldn't let me ride on the running board that day.
I loved to do that and feel the wind in my hair.
I'd sing "Off we go into the wild blue yonder"
and pretend that I was a pilot, or at least a stewardess.

When we got to town, I pet Lassie and we went into the dark, cool theater
smelling of popcorn and old men, and I fell asleep.
I woke up with a headache and felt cranky.
"I want to go," I whispered. "It's almost over," he said.
We left the movie early and went to the town diner.
I had a vanilla ice cream soda and Uncle Joe had a piece of apple pie.

When we got home, I was still cranky, unhappy and fussy.
The worst thing was that I was mean to Uncle Joe.
Uncle Joe, who had protected me from so much.
From my father's loud voice and big hand,
from my mother's pushing me to excel in school and everywhere else
and from my sister's teasing and harsh words.
"Leave her alone," was all that he had to say most of the time.
I went upstairs to bed early. They wouldn't let me take Buster with me.

During the night I thought I heard Mama crying
and a car crunch up the driveway.
In the morning the sun woke me up. My room had four windows
and two of them were full of sunshine.
When I started to get up, I heard someone coming up the stairs.
My door opened and it was Mrs. Jones from across the street.
"Sally, stay in bed for a minute. I have something to tell you.
Uncle Joe went to heaven last night."

Now I'm in my own home.
My yellow purse is on the dining room table.
The pen with cobalt blue ink is in my hand.
My dog goes to the backyard to find new smells.
I look old and substantial.
But I'm really that little girl, back in Goshen,
whose uncle just died.
The little girl who can't see colors any more, who can't taste food,
who can't stop crying.
Don't make me kiss him.
Don't make me say goodbye.
Don't make me go back there.
I can't look at that body in the living room.

I surround myself with barking dogs and Baroque music.
My hand keeps writing.
I loved a dying man, who smelled of the foundry and his victory garden.
I keep him alive by remembering him.
And some nights, if I've been very good,
and if I am very quiet, right before I go to sleep,
I can just remember the touch of his hand on my shoulder.

My Life

I am choking on my life.
I regurgitate it.
Nothing goes down.
Nothing goes away.

It's always there.
Grimy, grimy bits
of malicious behavior
pulsing in my body and brain.

He swoops down.
Takes me away.
Fondles me, feels me,
fucks me.
"It's ok. You're good.
Really good.
A good girl."
That's what they always say:
"A good girl."

I puke all over him. I puke.
I bite his hand. He screams.
Punches me. I roll into a ball.
Push myself away from him.

I open my eyes and peek out.
Move my pinky finger and right big toe.
I am here. He's gone. Gone to market.

The repugnant venom in me disgorges. Erupts.
I am huge. Gigantic. Spewing crap all around.
I stink. Smell of sulphur and shit.
My pink body grimed with excrement.

Want to fuck me now?

Mother

We didn't fit, you and me—
the suffocating mother and the stifled child.
Now I am the mother.
I decide who I am.

I am birthing myself.
With each stroke of the blue pen
I am becoming more alive.

You never wanted to get rid of me.
You contained me and wouldn't let me go.
I was always too big, too much for you.

As I write this, I know it's not true.
You didn't try to kill me.
I was too big for your small body.
I didn't fit and you couldn't let me go.

I need to be let go of.
I need to be on my own.
It's all done with words.
Killer words.

THE FLIPPING WIDOW

Are you sure that a floor cannot also be a ceiling?

M. C. Escher

My One and Only

I'm alone again, all by myself. I am my one and only. The last time I was alone, I found out that I was an unmarried woman in the eyes of the law. I wasn't single since I'd already been married. I was a divorcée. I would have rather been single.

This time I'm alone because I'm a widow—a word which I despise. I'm clumped in with the widows and orphans in the Bible, pitiful creatures who need to be taken care of by Deacons, and I have yet to find a Deacon to take care of me. Or the word is associated with black widow spiders whose sting can be fatal. I love spiders and have myself used many pieces of toilet paper to carry them to the back yard. What could they have hoped to have found in my tub?

The word widow to me is either a blubbering mass of incompetent sighs, tears and confusion or it's full of poisonous venom. I don't want to be either, but I'll take the latter for now. If I hear one more "sorry for your loss" from another stranger sitting in Chickasha, Oklahoma, or Mumbai, India, some stranger, who could care less and is reading a script, while they're telling me how much money I owe, or how little money I'll be getting, I'll—take your pick—scream—tear my hair out—kill myself.

At his death, everyone said it was "his time," "a blessing," "he didn't have to suffer," "the doctors did their best," "you did your best," "he's at peace."

For me, it was like losing an arm. It was so final, so sharp, so empty. There was no rewind, no trail, no path to him. I didn't have a god to take me to the underworld like Orpheus. The oxygen had been sucked out of my life.

The early days were difficult. I remember them in flashes. Joey, his dog, looking for him and going out to the garage to find him. The empty bed in the morning. His red car in the garage.

Then there was the obscene (to me) Memorial service held in a beautiful setting on a beautiful day. There was plenty of food and drink. I think I remember champagne. It seemed like a wedding when I wanted sackcloth and ashes. It was a wedding and I was the bride and there was no groom. It was too soon. He wasn't really dead yet. Nobody knew that it takes time to die. Just because he's not in a room doesn't mean that he's dead. He could have been at Costco picking up household supplies. Just because he's not at the kitchen table for breakfast reading the paper, doesn't mean he's dead. He could have gone early to the farmers market. Just because he's not in bed at night, next to me, doesn't mean he's dead. He could have been on a short business trip. It takes time to let someone die; especially if it's someone you love and have lived with for thirty years.

Everyone seemed so big and talked at the top of their voice. "Do this, do that, take this [a Xanax]." "It was a blessing," again. "Sorry for your loss," again, "Don't sell the house," again "Sell the house." And they always had me writing checks for the chairs, for the food, for the Rabbi. I didn't think I really needed a Rabbi, since we were married by a minister wearing dark glasses. I complied. I did what I was told to do.

After six P.M. they all disappeared and I was left alone with the dogs and TV. Thank God for Wimbledon.

Death is not a good playmate. I do not recommend the dying game. Like war, it is not healthy for children or other living things.

The Flipping Widow

This is my first chance to write
since he passed away on May 31st.
The same day Louise Bourgeois died.
I'd been reading her and went to her show at MOCA,
The one with the big sculpture of the spider taking care of her family.
One of her quotes was: "Art, art is the guarantee of sanity."
Now I'm a widow.
I've never been a flipping widow before.

I do not want to bring death into this room,
this writing room, looking out on a small garden
bound by the garage wall covered with creeping fig.
I do not want to be the knowing one.
I do not want to be one.
The spider taking care of everyone.

I am sad and grieving
as I see the flowers
moving in the breeze.
I feel his death in my stomach.

Today it came to me.
Today he came to me.

As long as I am here in this writing room,
facing the creeping fig, there is no death.
The sky is gray. The wind is rising.
The leaves flutter and I watch, remembering.

Remembering him petting the dogs.
Remembering him coming through the garage, carrying his briefcase.
Remembering him peeling a carrot, nibbling on it, like a rabbit,
as he carried it though the house.

Now, I'm the widow, with her small garden,
and the words of my art guarantee my sanity.

My Kitchen

My husband and I lived in a house with a square kitchen.
In the middle of the kitchen was a round table.
We walked around it getting things out of the fridge,
clearing the table, putting things in the dishwasher.
The dogs sat and watched us, looking for food.

We wandered around in our designated orbits.
slowly, carefully, not touching.
each knowing where the other was going.
We had our chosen paths

We were careful to remain in our orbits
fearing the explosion, the explosion, should we touch.

Marvin

Things have appeared in the house
since you've been gone:
people with loud voices,
computers with apples on them,
children who mark the walls.

I don't know the meaning of your absence.
I don't know why you left.
I don't know who I am.

Every object is different.
Lacking, floating,
nothing belongs.

I miss your silence.

A Widow Dreams

He came to me in a dream last night,
not to me, but to his home, the bed.
He lay down and
fixed his pillows just right,
turned on his left side and slept.

I woke up looking for him
The bed sheets were neat
no impression, no smells
everything cold and empty.

Then I remembered.
In the middle of the night
a woman had come to
take him back where he belonged.

I still sleep only on my right side, in case.

Tomatoes

Marvin's tomatoes are done.
I will go out this afternoon and harvest the last of them.
He never got to taste one.
He admired them when they were green and young.
"Very promising," he said.

I saw the new movie about Glenn Gould
and I was surprised by his good looks and energy.
I had only heard him play.

Gould suffered and trusted doctors with their colored pills
and Latin names. The blue one for depression, the red for anxiety.
He died of a stroke at age fifty.

Marvin was no child prodigy or genius,
but he was alive, vital and read the *New York Times*
and the *New Yorker*. He kept up.
He, too, trusted doctors and their colored pills
with their fancy Latin names.

He, too, died in a hospital before his time.
The surgery, said the doctors, was a success.

Six Months after Marvin's Death

I sit in my room at my table.
The creeping fig is up to the roof of the garage.
The sun on the window pane
shows the marks from the rain.

The gray Swiss ball and the purple yoga mat
still guard the French doors.
Gracie snores, stretched out on the faded carpet
and my grandson, Vaughn, smiles at me from the picture frame.

The Silver Elephant

At first I mourned Marvin for what he did.
Now I mourn him for who he was.

I keep the small silver elephant that he gave me on my desk

At first I mourned Marvin for what he did.
Now I mourn him for who he was.

We were in Italy and stumbled upon an elephant statue
I told him how much I love elephants.

At first I mourned Marvin for what he did.
Now I mourn him for who he was.

His Death, the Buddhists and Me

Four days after his death I went back to the Buddhists—the Thursday morning sitting group that I had been attending off and on for about five years. I had told the leader, Trudy, about Marvin's death and she told me to come, just come.

I did just that. Got up, got in the car, came into the room and sat down. That's what meditation is: You sit. You sit with other people that sit. Most of them are on cushions on the floor with their knees crossed and their backs straight. They sit with their eyes closed and their backs straight. The women often wrap a pashmina or a colored stole around their shoulders and the men just sit. I sit in a chair since my knees no longer work that way. The group meets at 7 A.M. and sits. There are the occasional sleepers. I've never heard anyone snore.

So I entered into silence, a silence which was different from the silence I had been living in at home without Marvin. I have found that there are many kinds of silence, many different words for it, like the different words Eskimos use for snow. There's silence, quiet, hushed, noiseless, still, tranquil, rest, repose, death.

I'm not the best Buddhist in the world. I don't know that I am really a Buddhist. I can never remember the four noble truths that lead to the eight-fold path. I remember the first truth—suffering exists. I am acquainted with suffering and grief, as Isaiah predicted about Jesus in the Bible. I knew that I needed the solace of silence, group silence.

We sat for forty minutes. The leader hit the metal singing bowl, three times and we listened to the reverberations fall into silence and then bowed for respect. The leader, Trudy, delivered a dharma talk. I'm not sure what dharma means either—I just chalk it up to life.

At some point, Trudy mentioned my situation—Marvin's sudden death and my widowhood. I was embarrassed and wanted to hide under my pashmina, I think I was using the green one.

The reaction of the Buddhists was odd. It wasn't a simple "poor you." It was more like a brave you, strong you, lucky you. You are close to death. You are touching mystery.

Nobody came out and said that. It was what I felt coming from then. I felt like a hero, a warrior: I felt that I was blessed by death and fortunate to have been given this experience. I felt that I had gravitas.

People came up and hugged me. The next week some gave me poems, they had written themselves. I did not hear one "sorry for your loss." I felt their willingness to accept me and to journey with me. They weren't afraid of me and my proximity to death. I didn't see any pity in their eyes and heard no "shoulds."

It was peculiar. I felt peculiar. I am quick and sensitive and used to being the outsider. The other. And it seemed to me that in their eyes I was the hero. A hero for the first time in my life. I thought I would be shunned, demeaned, categorized. Instead I felt respected and maybe even honored.

Now, almost a year later. I still don't understand. I keep sitting, keep silent, keep still, keep wrapping myself in different colors, listening to nothing.

His Death, the Christians and Me

"He's in a better place."
"You're in our prayers."
"He didn't have to suffer."
"Be thankful."
"It's God's will."
"Time heals all wounds."
"Sometimes it's hard to see, but God is all-knowing and merciful."

The problem to me is that they were all trying to justify death, to put it in a neat package. To give it the gift of reason. I'm finding that death is not reasonable. It would have been reasonable for Marvin to live a few more years. It would have been reasonable for Marvin to die in his sleep. It would have been reasonable for Marvin to die in his garden like in *The Godfather*, his favorite movie.

The Christians anthropomorphize death like Disney does animals. I'm surprised they haven't named it, like Fred, George, or Gertrude, or maybe they have: "God's will." Marvin didn't believe in him or her, so why should he follow His or Her will.

Maybe Marvin would have traded a little suffering so he could say goodbye or pet Joey one more time. Or tell me when to water the plants, put the medicine on the dogs, and change the filter in the furnace. Suffering might have been a good trade.

In the Christian community I do not feel like a hero. I am a widow. I am the other. I am the odd person out. I'm the loner. Poor me. Poor you. "I am so sorry for your loss."

The most hated phrase of all.

There is nothing worse than being the recipient of anyone's pity, whether it comes from a priest, a clerk, or a friend.

Until I went through it and I am still going through it. Trying to understand what it means and who I am after thirty years of being half of something. Struggling with aloneness, silence, responsibility, decisions, emptiness, sorrow, dogs, shopping, bank clerks, bills, plumbing, the boredom of oneness. No one to defer to. No one to blame.

There is no pattern that I have found. I am forming my own and I cannot see the structure. I am the black widow spider, who doesn't know how to make her web.

It's Been a Year—Almost

I've heard that the Jews commemorate the one-year anniversary of someone's death by having a special ceremony—Yahrtzeit; and they burn a Yahrtzeit candle for twenty-four hours. It's a time dedicated to remembrance. I think I should celebrate and remember myself getting through this year. This first year of being a widow.

Marvin was never a big one for anniversaries, birthdays, holidays. He wasn't a celebratory kind of guy. I know that he just endured most of the ones that I promulgated.

I am going to have a gathering and there will be a remembrance of Marvin. His son gave me what's left of his ashes and they're in the hall closet and we'll take that opportunity to put them in the back garden. Marvin loved the garden. Last year the tomatoes that he had planted were just beginning to appear on the vines. There's a rose that he liked, "Just Joey." It's an unusual salmon color and has a big blossom with little scent. We bought it for Joey, his favorite dog. So that will be good. We'll have a little ceremony, bury the ashes and then order in Bryan County Texas Barbecue, which Marvin loved and we will be sure to order the homemade peach cobbler for desert.

What about me? What do I get as I celebrate in this year of his death? I think that death is over-rated as a companion. It might be sexist, but I think of death as a man. Not someone old or haggard, certainly not someone with a scythe. I haven't seen one of them around here, ever. But I see him as nondescript—someone not worth a second look. Not bad-looking exactly, but not someone you would want to linger on. And you definitely would not want to lock eyes with him.

He's been ok around the house. He usually leaves the room as I enter. I've almost caught him hanging around in Marvin's office. And I think he's the one who messed up the computer. I doubt that he has much of a sense of humor.

It's very quiet here right now. I can hear the clock ticking each time the second hand moves and the children playing in the distance. The wind is moving the birch tree leaves and they cast shadows on the wall in the late afternoon sun. So this is a perfect time, a quiet time for him, for death. Even though he's been around for a year, we haven't been formally introduced.

I think he's overstayed his visit a wee bit. I don't want to hurt his feelings. He's been most benign. A time comes for all things to end and I think it's time for us to part until it's my time.

I think I'll order an extra helping of the peach cobbler, just in case he comes back sooner than expected.

Yahrzeit

Yesterday was Marvin's deathday.
The one-year anniversary of his death.
A friend brought over a 24-hour candle
available at any supermarket.
We poured a glass of wine,
said the blessing, lit the candle and toasted Marvin.
The candle's still burning this morning.

It also marks one year
of my being alone without him.
I hope he will say: "Good job."
"You took good care of the house and Gracie.
You've made it through the first year."

I have decided that now
I want my own one-year anniversary.
A time to celebrate a new life.
A life lived alone, a life lived well.

AN ASSEMBLAGE OF POETS

Art is the guarantee of sanity.

Louise Bourgeois

Jane Kenyon—I

It's just dawn here in Santa Monica.
I look out at a grey blue sky silhouetting the trees.
Our green is different from yours but our dogs are the same.
I treasure your words and read them sparingly, afraid they'll wear out.
I am older than you. It will always be that way.
You died before I knew you. You died before the wrinkles, came.
You died too soon, poisoned by your own blood, playing the cancer dance
of tests, scans, and biopsies, aided by your doctors,
dressed in green and white.
Your words are still fresh, vibrant and full of lilac, saffron and goldenrod.
I know bits of your life, how the wind stings when it comes over the ice
and what it's like to walk the dog on a soggy road after days of rain.
I have no woods but I have four birches in front of my home and a dog.
I am alone, no one to laugh with, sleep with, sing with.
I watch my skin change color, texture and shape. We all have our time.

Jane Kenyon—II

Those doctors in their green and white clothes, told you:
"No more. There's nothing else we can do.
It's time for you to die.
We're out of false promises."

Could you feel the fear any longer? Or was it tapped out?
Was it a relief? A relief to just be able to go home?
Go home to Eagle Pond. Go home to the dog.
Go home to your bed and die.

I look out at the white flowers moving in the breeze.
It's one of those days when the wind comes up
and it gets cooler in the afternoon.
The dogs are asleep at my feet.
Just an ordinary day.
Nothing special.

The question is why. Why am I here? And not you?

My dogs are nothing special—a small Jack Russell and a rescue.
Maybe it's the gray-and-white mockingbird—
The one who just came back.

He just came back to his perch on the top of the telephone pole.
He has many songs to enchant his future mate.
He sings as he flies straight into the air to display his magnificent body.

I listen and wish it was for me.
Maybe someday it will be.

I would be happy to sing and dance
on the top of a telephone pole
if I could find my true love.

I'm too old for this.

I'm nothing special.

A Letter to All of Them, but Mostly to Jane

Jane, I've loved this time with you, getting to know more of your life,
but it's time for me to leave you for now.

I've become obsessed with you, how you lived and mostly how you died.

I love it that you called the stand holding the IV
that pumped the poison into your blood "Igor."

I love it that shortly after you moved to Eagle Pond,
you didn't want to leave.
You knew your home when you saw it.

I love it that you worried about your weight
and that you named your dog Gus
and noted the colors of Mt. Kearsarge
and that dark purple lilacs were your favorite.

And I'm reading all the letters that Hayden Carruth sent to you
during your illness, sharing his life between poetry readings
and his own illnesses and getting a dog
after having a house filled with two cats.

There is much more that I want to know about you,
but it's enough for now.

It's time for me to get back to my own life, my own dog.

I'll be leaving here soon—this spring or summer.
I call my home "The Birches,"
which is presumptuous for a Santa Monica cottage
built for Douglas Aircraft workers after the war.
It's been remodeled so many times
there are only shadows of the original house.
Two rooms seem to be original—
in one the baseboard doesn't quite fit the wall.
In the other, the closet door is askew.

As I sit here I hear the children playing in the park.
The planes are silent today. It's not a good day for flying.
Gracie's snoring in her favorite chair.

The clock on my desk ticks. I think of time—your time, my time.
Hayden knew his time was coming when he wrote you that year,
never expecting a reply.

I don't know when my time is coming. I know it will be quiet.
I hope to have a snoring dog nearby.

Jane and the Poet

I know how you met him.
You submitted many poems.
He picked the one that was not generic.
It all started from one poem.

I want to find that one poem for myself.
The one that will say: "She notices things."

I want that life:
The one full of poetry, the cats and the dog.
The one full of trees, mud and country air.

I have some of it now—
my small garden
with Gracie snoring at my feet.

We both know there's no holding on.
The time came for you and it will come for me.

Penultimate Letter to Jane

I would have loved to be at your funeral at the small country church
in New Hampshire in April our cruelest month.

It was just Spring—the day was warm for that time of year in
     New England.

An assemblage of poets—Sharon Olds, Galway Kinnell, Charles Simic,
Robert Bly, Robert Pinsky, Louis Simpson, Donald Hall.

I went to two memorials this year—that's what we call them now—
one for my husband and one for a young man, like you, who died of cancer.

Does it make any difference what people die of? Does it make any
     difference
how old they were? Do we care what they did in life?

At the dying time, the just dead time we don't care. I don't care.
The dead are gone. A torn page in a magazine at the doctor's office.

I search for them, for him, for Marvin, when I am awake and dreaming—
looking for that part of myself that I will never find again.
If I could just focus my eyes better, or turn my head quicker, I know he'd
     be there.

Why It's Time for Me to Say Goodbye to Jane, Hayden, Yevgeny and Anna

I don't want to look backwards anymore.
I'm tired of grieving. That other life was so long ago.
There is no god to take me to where the dead are.
No app on my Smartphone, no voice in my car, or whisper in my ear.

I might have been one of you.
I might have been born a man.
I might have been born in Michigan.

I am here now in my bedroom with the French doors,
Jane's book near my left elbow. The magnifying glass
on top of my notebook. The dog snoring at my feet.
I see her reflection in the door.

My day was full of people and places.
Bob's Market, Trader Joe's, Coldwell Banker.
A client from Hawaii.
The saleswoman in the Marina.
Each on his own path like pinballs in a machine.
Everyone buying,
everyone selling,
everyone, touching,
everyone trying to fill the void.

Sergei Yesenin—I

Sergei, you are dead, stone cold dead.
How much blood did it take to write that last poem?
Did you have enough? What about breath?
It takes breath to breathe a poem.
Did you read it out loud? So that you could hear it?
The sound of it.

You have missed out on the growing old part.
The part that's a series of small good-byes.
Everything narrows, darkens, mutates.

You have beautiful hands, smooth and strong.
Mine are lined, wrinkled, age-marked, with veins exposed.
I'm staying at the party longer, staying for the last drink, last kiss,
sucking on every morsel
that this life
gives me.

My green creeping fig has taken over the garage.
The red of the crown of thorns is as bright as blood.
Soon the hydrangeas and roses will come.
And the dead are with me—my dead
Uncle Joe, Marvin, Buster, Joey, Mom, Dad, Aunt Sis.
They are here with me, waiting.

Sergei Yesenin—II

Questions....

I know of suicides here in sunny Santa Monica.
A 21-year-old jumped from his father's building.
A 17-year-old jumped to her death across the street from Samo High.
A 15-year-old hung herself in her room with
her black and white panda on her bed.
Our young are killing themselves.

What did you know, Yevgeny? I hope I can call you that.
Why did you do it—take the turn to darkness that good night.
When did a baby's smile or a dog wagging his tail
stop giving you reason to live?
When did you stop feeling the brisk chill of an early fall day
or the last rays of sun?

As I write this to you, my brown and white dog
patrols the back yard looking for prey.
Those youths, what happened to them? One played baseball.
The other was an artist. The girl had beaucoup friends.

When you opened your body to release the blood
to write your last poem, how did you know how much blood was required?
Did the amount of blood limit the length of the poem?
Did you run out of words first, or breath, or blood?

I only ask because there are so many of us who want to stay here,
determined to suck up every smile, every flower, every word.

If, like Christ, you return,
would you do it again?

To Donald Hall

We're still here, the two of us, the survivors.
You, not quite alone, still in Eagle Pond.
Me, alone, still in Santa Monica for now.

You know the language of cancer:
Brainscans, delirium, intensifications,
leukemia, MRIs. You learned it all.

You were surrounded by death.
Doctors and death.
Hope and despair.
You knew the outcome from the first phone call.

They doctors did what they could, chemo, ports,
a marrow transplant, more medicines with long names.
Those fifteen months of fearing the worst and doing your best.

My loss was quicker, a clot to the heart.
An explosion. Boom! He's gone.
Nothing like the slow drip of an IV.

Some days I think I was lucky.
Some days I think you were.
Some days I just don't know.

Jim Harrison

I was awakened at four this morning
by a shiny crescent moon in a dark sky.
There were no starlights, starbrights.
I stayed awake until it raced away from me,
leaving dreams of green stalactites and baby elephants.

I'm writing to you Jim, you at 35, with two young children
and a bag full of cocaine and psilocybin and cheap burgundy.
I did all of that, except for the cocaine, which made me too much me.
We had "blue flats" straight from San Francisco in the Oregon Mountains.
I opened my eyes and the tree was made of wrought iron.
Indian thunderbirds and Swedish peacocks made up my skin.
I saw it all brother, every bit. It was all opened to me,
tempered by Gallo, always Gallo.

We did all that and neither one of us died.
You keep writing and I keep dreaming.

Leaving Jane

On this last day of February, this last bright and sunny day.
This last day with Mozart playing,
I am leaving you, Jane. You are dead and I am alive.
You died young, full of so much promise.
I will die old. Even old people have promise.
I'm at my desk hearing Gracie snore, older with each breath.
I mean the both of us.
How many breaths do I have left and how many words?

You suffered from depression.
I suffer from anxiety, depression's other face.
I am familiar with fear. I have to stop thinking of you.
You are too real to me,
an invisible friend, my only companion besides Gracie.
I have to, want to, go on finding my own words,
writing my own songs, listening to our breaths.

I mean, the both of us. Mine and Gracie's.

Me, Jane, Gus and Gracie

I was awakened this morning by the slice of moon
waiting over my left shoulder to be seen.
It was there to remind me that we all have our own path.
His to keep out of the way of the sun.
I saw him leave over the right skylight.

It's time for me to leave.
It's time for me to leave Jane
and Gus, the rescue dog that charmed her,
her "designated optimist."

Jane's words are careful, rich, lovely, delicate,
pored over, concise, evocative.
Mine are scribblings, rushed to the page,
illegible, brash, coarse, pushed out like unplanned babies.

Jane had Gus with the big tail and ever-present smile.
I have Gracie with a stumpy tale and nose pressed to the ground.

My creeping fig juts out from the garage wall.
It will soon take over the yard.

The sun chases the moon.
Gracie chases rats.
I chase words.

FROM NOW & THEN ON

No one saves us but ourselves. No one can and no one may. We ourselves must walk the path.

Buddha

The Visitor

My room, my desk, Haydn on the radio.
The creeping fig is up and over the roof.
My pen is running out of ink.
I'll have to find out where to get a new one.
Like many things this past year,
the only remaining stationery store has closed.

It feels good to be writing again.
Gracie's snoring on the bed.
I love this moment.
Violins and Gracie's snores,
who could ask for anything more? I'm happy.

I saw an insect the other day in my backyard.
She was new to me. She was a dragonfly.
I haven't seen one for a long time.
The unusual thing about her was that she was all head-to-wings
     shades of brown.
It was as if she had her own stylist who matched everything.
Her wings—she had four of them—were gossamer-thin
and her round head had a brown cap with a tan streak around it.
The rest of her body was also brown and went to shades of mahogany,
nut brown, chocolate and taupe.

She was munching on the stem of an aloe plant I got years ago from
     Trader Joe's.
It was now way too big for the house.
She let me get very close. I didn't seem to bother her.
She would take occasional breaks from eating and fly around the plant.
She made a soft buzzing sound when she flew.
I didn't have a camera so I had to preserve her in my mind.

Other dragonflies that I've seen have been multi-colored.
This one was elegant and polished in her muted shades of brown outfit
and also was very sure of herself and committed to her meal.
There was no rushing her in her enjoyment.

The unique thing about her was that she was so delicate
and so strong at the same time. That bug was hungry.

She was phosphorescent and diaphanous.
A gift, a treasure for my eyes alone.

I wondered if anyone were watching me as I watched her.
She is so refined and composed, and I am so unfinished and rough around
    the edges.
She shimmers and is light on her feet.
I plod. I shuffle, hold on to things to make my way.
But, I can see, and I can remember,
and I can record beauty.
That I can do.

When I entered the house and returned to my desk,
my *Mira Calligraphiae Monumenta* was open to Folio 76—The Dragonfly,
a common household pest.

Vacation

I had forgotten the Fall.
I had forgotten the Fall in New England.
I had forgotten the trees and their colors,
remembering only the gold and oranges.
I had forgotten the audacious scarlet.
I had forgotten the pumpkins, garlands
and straw men outlining each doorway.
I had forgotten the geese in the early morning fog,
taking off over the lake in perfect formation.

I had forgotten the steepled churches, their graveyards surrounded
       by green.
I had forgotten the town square.
I had forgotten the black and white cows,
and the hay stacks strewn over fields,
the barns and the silos.

I had forgotten Uncle Dick's berry patch
and Aunt Gus' yellow house.
I had forgotten the scary picture
of my Swedish grandmother hanging over the mantel.
I had forgotten the sun porch filled with old magazines
and the rocking chair facing the street.

And me.

I had forgotten me.

Windows

I love looking out of windows.
There's something about being here, not there.
I can see how pieces fit, what birds do.
How flowers grow, colors change, wind moves.
The creeping fig has taken over the garage wall.
Just as the lines have taken over my face.

All the News That's Fit to Print but Who Wants to Read It?

It all started last Friday. I co-lead a group at a church every week. We pray in silence for twenty minutes and I read a poem and then a reading from Julian of Norwich, a 14th-century English mystic. The idea is to get together and see what this wise woman from the past has to say to us now.

I was in a hurry to get to the meeting, running late and I grabbed a poem to read, "Wild Geese," by Mary Oliver. I just skimmed it, I didn't really read it. It had the words "wild geese" in the title and I thought it was about nature and our planet. I told the group that it's a poem that speaks of the beauty of nature that is a gift to us all. It's all there for the looking. The poem is a transformative piece full of the outrageous glory that surrounds us. That's what I said, which was all wrong

Georgia said, "That's one of my favorite poems."

Lydia said, "Roses are my favorite flowers."

Karen said, "I love the smell of night-blooming jasmine."

The piece that I read from Julian spoke of God loving us as a child. A God who is willing to wrap himself around us as a piece of clothing or a blanket. A God who is full of love for us as a mother to her child.

Nobody had much to say about Julian's words. Especially me. I came to the meeting upset about Fukushima. Upset about the nuclear plant spewing radiation throughout Japan, our planet and the universe. Upset about the seemingly unending nature of this disaster and upset and fearful of the Japanese government's failure to disclose the severity of the incident.

"It's hard for me to think of the beauty of God's love when we just got the news of Fukushima. I can't believe that this is happening in Japan, the country of Hiroshima and Nagasaki and the Enola Gay. It doesn't make any sense that the people would let this happen to them and by their own hand. There are survivors of the atomic bombs still alive today. Don't they have a voice?"

Cynthia said, "I'm sure it will be contained. It's over in Japan. It won't affect us."

Laura said, "It might, we don't know yet."

"Yes, I said, I'm sure radiation is on our way over to us now, even as we sit here, praying."

Laura said, "And what about Chernobyl? That happened twenty-five years ago and there's still radiation there. I think I read somewhere that nobody can live there for 1,000 years."

"Yeah, I said. I lived in a condo next door to a family who lived there. The father was some sort of engineer and one of their two boys was really affected by radiation sickness. I read that they're giving tours of Chernobyl now, like Disneyland. It costs $150 and you can rent out Geiger counters."

Frank, our co-leader and a priest, finally spoke, "Sarah, you seem pretty upset and so am I. How about we take another look at the poem? I think that there's more there. Let's reread it and listen again. Sharon, why don't you give it a read?"

Sharon read it and I sat and listened. When Sharon finished reading, everyone was silent.

I said, "I'm sorry. After listening to Sharon's reading I realized that this was not just a nature poem, but one about redemption and despair. And that we don't have to be perfect and good to fit in with the nature of things. That we are part of this vast, beautiful and wild universe and we have our place. I'm so sorry, I apologize to you all for bringing something that I haven't really read. I was in a hurry and just grabbed it."

"No worries, Sarah, it's a great poem," Frank said, I'm sure we've all done the same kind of thing. It's an amazing poem, and if you think about it, it relates to Julian's words about God's love covering us like a blanket, wherever we are, no matter how lonely."

"I was happy we got to hear it again," said Cynthia.

"We have to move on if we're going to get out of here by twelve. It's time for Sunday's Gospel reading and noonday prayers" said Frank.

I left the meeting feeling upset, exposed, like an x-ray. I still haven't recovered from the oil spill in the gulf, or the Exxon-Valdez spill in Alaska. And now Japan.

The next day Washington got the country into another war. This one against Muammar Gaddafi, another madman in the Mideast. Another war, when we still have two going. Another war against a madman that we had befriended. Another war against a madman—it's like fucking a snake, nothing good can come from it. Although I did just see a movie where a woman was fucked by a fish, a catfish at that. It seemed to be working for her.

Later in the day, I heard that radiation had gotten into milk and spinach that had been shipped to Tokyo. This means that it's in the soil and in the cows. Harmless cows chewing their radioactive cud.

Afterwards I went to Trader Joe's. They were out of zucchini and I asked a worker for some from the back. She said: "Do you want organic, or regular?" I said: "I don't care as long as it's not radioactive." Two women looked at me and smiled.

The Path

I walk, one foot in front of the other.
I walk on a dirt path.
I walk around a golf course.
I am lucky.

I see squirrels, birds, golf balls.
dogs, people. I hear them talking.
I walk, looking at foot prints.
I walk, counting dogs.

When I take Gracie, she walks in circles,
head down, searching for prey.
She has never found anything.
And I am happy.
Just one foot at a time.

The Crows

The crows had their usual meeting in the early morn,
assembled on the wires behind my house.
They blared the usual complaints
and changed positions at random.

They usually meet at the golf course,
but today was special. It was for me.
A call to get up. Wake up. Go. Do.
We want you awake. Hurry up.

The great pacific garbage patch is coming.
We're happy. We love it.
But it's not for you.
Your earth is slipping away.

You call us a murder of crows.
We'll show you.
You'll be the one hanging on a wire
and then we will crow.

The City

I opened the newspaper this morning—no I didn't have to open it.
The news was spread on the front page.
Fifty new earthquake faults in California—
still the smog capital of the country.
I chose to live here. It's all my fault.
I should have stayed in New York—the city.
My children would be New Yorkers and talk like me.
I'd still be married to my first husband and would be rich,
living in our apartment with parquet floors in Brooklyn Heights.

I followed my family out here—how crazy was that?
I wouldn't have had a morning like this,
awakening to earthquakes and smog.
I wouldn't have had to take the old dog outside to pee.
I wouldn't have had to take the young dog out front to get the paper.
I would be in the city reading *The New York Times* and doing the crossword.
Listening to WQXR in my apartment with the parquet floors.
A widow because he died. A widow with two cats.
Cats are easier than dogs in the City.

Dreams

I have no place,
no peace,
no hint of solace,
no comfort, consolation,
no nest,
no teddy-bear man
or woman.
No analyst's couch
in a dark cave of a room.

The world is too light, too bright.
I need shadows and candlelight.
Flickerings that give subtlety
and dimension to existence.
There are no caves,
no dark holes accessible to me.
I like the underside of things.
The words not said.
The peace of silence.
I exist in bruising daylight.
A smiling apparition of myself.

The Boys

The boys came over yesterday, chatty, talking, piping up.
One blonde—a slim Viking—the other taupe,
with hazel, almond shaped eyes.
They are ten and very sure of themselves.
Sure of their magical gifts.
They can talk to animals, and it's easy.
I say, I talk to my dogs all the time.
No, they say. You don't talk out loud, you think it to them.
You think something really good and they'll do it.

They went outside to find more dogs to talk to—mine were sleeping.
They came back: "How did it go?" I asked.
Good they said, except for the dogs next door.
They wouldn't come close enough to the fence.
We tried thinking to squirrels but their minds are full of nuts.

They went outside again.
I saw them standing on my split rail fence, hanging on a tree limb.
Soon they were back—"Can we have water for the tree, we want to thank
it for letting us hang on it."
I gave them two glasses full of water which they placed next to the tree.
They tried to talk to the crows.
The boys tell me: "They're really smart birds."
One boy said: "they're ravens."

What will they be up to the next time they come?

The next day their mothers called.
They had lied about not having any homework.

A New Day

It will be a clean year
because of the rain.

My sins are washed away
along with my memories.

I am wet with wonder
and moist with dew.

Sealed with the oil
of enduring love.

The Big Red Dog

    two men walk on the boardwalk holding

hands, smiles

   on their faces.

the red dog lumbers beside them,
                                    a goofy look on

his face.

the men stop
      try on sunglasses
           look in mirrors
   look at each other

too silly
        too big   outrageous

the big dog lies down
          puts his head on his paws and dreams his dreams.

the three of them walk along,

two of them holding hands,

the other one dreaming.

The Splitter-Upper

Soon after I married I realized that I had chosen this husband because I was sure no one else would want him. We were at a coffee house in Cambria after an abbreviated honeymoon and had finished breakfast. Or I had and was watching him finish his eggs and bacon. He ate and ate and ate, looking at the food and table and not at me. When necessary, he slurped his coffee. We didn't talk, not even small talk. I've never been able to hold onto men, starting with my first boyfriend in college. He was stolen away from me by a waitress at the off-campus diner. Her name was Winnie. She wasn't very pretty or smart but had nice boobs. Not only did I lose Teddy, but that diner made the best banana splits and I could never go back there again.

No need to recount my long sad history. If my boyfriends weren't stolen from me, it was usually because they were already married. I finally wised up when I realized that one of my lovers who was cheating on his wife, was cheating on me.

They say that he who lives may learn and I finally realized that rather than looking for the best the opposite sex had to offer, I'd do much better with a reject or "also-ran." Someone who'd been used up and spit out. Someone that not even Winnie would want.

So I found him, Fred. He'd been married twice before me and one of his wives had turned gay after they split up and the other was a three-hundred pounder. He wasn't ugly, but definitely not worth a second look. He was also not un-intelligent—I at least needed someone with whom I could have a decent dinner conversation and introduce to my friends.

I did notice that he was on the depressed side. But I figured that this might balance out my high-anxiety strain. And besides, Eeyore was one of my favorite childhood characters.

So we got married and we lived a normal boring life and with the help of a few shrinks along the way, eked out a marriage that would pass for normal. Fred continued to be depressed and low in energy, but we created a jigsaw puzzle of our lives and we both knew where the pieces fit.

Until, until, until he quit working and was around the house all the time. All the time, 24/7. And he slept. The whole time. Morning, noon and night. After breakfast, lunch and dinner. Not only did he sleep, but he snored. That's how I'd know where he was when I came home. I'd go to the place with the loudest snore. The dogs snore too, but not so loud. I couldn't stand living with him.

We tried everything for his condition. We consulted all sorts of doctors—more shrinks, neurologists, acupuncturists, otolaryngologists. We did sleep studies, nothing helped. I was doomed to live with a man who was like a piece of furniture that had to be moved at different intervals during the day.

One morning when I was alone in my office and online, I saw an article about a practice that was common in Japan. And it sounded interesting. If you were in a situation that you couldn't stand and needed to change, you hired a Wakaresaseys, or splitter-upper, and for a fee they would split up the relationship—do whatever needs to be done to break it up.

Wow, I thought, this would be perfect for me and Fred. If I could hire someone to steal him away from me, I'd be alone and not have him sleeping around the house all the time. I could have the house to myself and listen to music and watch TV without being interrupted by those terrible snores.

I found an agency after much diligent internet surfing. I explained my situation and they agreed to take Fred on for a fee. They guaranteed me much happiness and had a lot of happy clients. The fee seemed nominal considering the potential results.

There was only one problem, how was I going to get him out of the house so the splitter-upper could find him? It took me a while, but I figured it out. Our neighborhood is littered with coffee houses, and I harangued, bitched, bothered and annoyed Fred so much that he promised to go out of the house at least once a day for coffee. I suggested that maybe he should do it around the same time of day, so it would be a nice routine for him. We settled on late afternoon, around 4:30.

I contacted the agency, told them of the arrangement and paid the first installment. Nothing much happened the first week or so, but after a while, I did notice a subtle shift in his behavior. He didn't seem to be sleeping quite as much, and he started talking. Not much, of course. He stopped complaining about leaving the house and even seemed to look forward to it.

I was feeling pretty smug. The agency said everything was going well and it wouldn't be long before he would be willing to separate and leave the house. I was ecstatic.

After a while I noticed that he came home later and later, and sometimes he was even gone in the morning, and then he started going for walks and exercising, something he would never do in all our years together. He was becoming a new version of himself.

One morning, as I was leaving for work, he said "Ginny, can we talk? I need to talk to you."

I put down my keys and sunglasses and looked at him. Really looked at him. He was a different person. He looked years younger. His skin was no longer damp and pasty. He had lost the bags under his eyes. He even had the start of a smile on his face. He seemed nervous; he was fidgeting with his napkin. Fred never fidgeted.

"What is it?" I said.

"I'm leaving, I know I said I never would and we'd never get a divorce, but I want to leave."

The splitter-upper had done her job, just what I wanted her to do. This was great. But how come I was so miserable? I felt gut-punched. My legs were weak; I had to lean against the counter for support. I was shocked by his words and my reaction.

"What do you mean you're leaving? You're leaving me and the dogs and the house? You're leaving?" I was nauseated and trying to keep a grip. "What happened?"

"I met someone," he said. "A really nice girl. We went to the coffee shop at the same time and started talking. She's really interested in what I have to say. And she laughs at my jokes. Nobody has ever done that."

"What does she look like?" I said.

"As I said, she's young and pretty and has straight black hair. She's Asian, but I don't know where she's from. She's very sweet." He smiled as he was telling me this.

"Look Fred, I can't talk about this now. I have to get to work, Mrs. Jacobs is coming in and we're writing an offer. I have to go. Can we talk more about this tonight at dinner? Please."

"Sure Ginny, I guess it can wait. See you later." He went back to his napkin.

I picked up my keys and sunglasses, went to the garage, opened the garage door, started the car, drove about a block, parked by the curb and phoned the agency.

The man I had talked to answered right away. "Hello, this is Mrs. Adams," I said. "What's going on? What is that woman doing to my husband? I want you to call her off. He's mine and I don't want anyone else having him. I want to split up the splitter-upper. I don't care how much it costs. What kind of a business do you run, anyway?"

"Excuse me," he said, "I'm sure we can reach some sort of accommodation that would be satisfactory for you. My name is Jonathon Ito and the lady in question will comply with your wishes. She has been a faithful employee for some years. What do you wish me to do?"

"Send her home where she came from as soon as possible. But, listen to this, my husband has a soft heart, so be sure to come up with a good story, family illness, death, something really significant, an old lover, maybe. Something that means that she will never return here and that her relationship with my husband is over forever. I will pay any necessary fees, including one-way travel expenses."

Mr. Ito and I had a lengthy conversation working out the details of Amy's (that's her name) breakup with my husband. He quoted me the price and we negotiated a little, but we both knew he had the upper hand.

At the end of the negotiating, I said, "OK, Mr. Ito, that amount seems a little high, but fair, and I have no choice. I'll get a cashier's check and send you a copy, but you won't get the original until my husband tells me that the relationship is definitely over and I see it in his eyes. And that could take a few weeks."

"But Mrs. Adams, that could take a long time. It could take months."

"Mr. Ito, if it doesn't happen, if my husband's eyes don't change towards me in a month, I'll send you the check. You have my word."

"How about sending me the amount of her airfare now so I don't have to put out any unnecessary money?"

"You're a tough negotiator, Mr. Ito, but I can see your point. I'll have it messengered to you this morning. And I'll also send you the check, but hold it until I let you know that the eagle has landed."

My heart was beating hard when I hung up and my hands hurt since I was gripping the steering wheel so tightly. I hoped that he was a man of his word and that the splitter-upper would go back where she came from. But what was I going to do with Fred? The new Fred. The one that I wanted back? *One step at a time,* I told myself, *one step at a time.*

I went to work, wrote up the contract for Mrs. Jacobs, put the package together, emailed it and called the listing agent to look out for it. Thank God it wasn't a multiple offer situation.

I couldn't get my mind off of Fred, how good he looked and what good shape he was in and maybe we could do things together and have some fun and sex, what about that? What about that? It's been so long for me, I don't know that I've got it anymore. First things first. What would Fred like? He always liked food. I can cook for him. Good food. I know what he likes. I can do that. Thank God I've stuck to Weight Watchers and the gym. I didn't let myself go. I left work early and went to Gelson's in the Palisades for some really good meat, vegetables and the hummus that Fred liked.

When I got home, he wasn't there. I changed clothes and started prepping for dinner. I couldn't make anything fancy that I knew he'd like since there was no time. Just appetizers, a good steak and baked potato and salad. No dessert, neither one of us needed that.

Fred got home late, around 7:30. I heard him walk into the living room. He stayed there. I left the kitchen and went to him.

"Hi, Fred, how's it going? I have a nice dinner ready to go when you're ready." Then I realized that he hadn't turned the lights on. I switched them on. He was sitting in his favorite brown chair. Just sitting, not looking at anything. One of the dogs was at his feet. "I had to go to the Palisades to drop off the offer and I've got some good eating ready to go. I have that tall-grass beef that you like."

"Ginny, just leave me alone. I'm not hungry."

"I thought you wanted to talk. I thought we could talk over dinner."

"I don't want to talk. I don't want to think. I don't know what happened."

A dog was on his lap and he was petting her ears, not looking at her, not looking at anything, just petting. "Ginny, just go away. Leave me alone."

"OK, I'll save everything for tomorrow. Just let me know when you want to talk."

I went to bed early. I felt a strange feeling in my stomach. I couldn't figure it out, I wasn't hungry, I wasn't sick, I just felt weird. In the middle of the night I woke up and realized what it was—I felt sorry for Fred.

Nothing much happened the next couple of days. Fred moped about the house, still not talking. I gave him as much space as I could, kept the good food going, filled the house with flowers, I hadn't bought any for a long time, and I just kept quiet. I still had that strange feeling in my stomach. He spent a lot of time in the living room with at least one of the dogs.

A day later I came home from work and was putting the groceries away, when Fred walked into the kitchen and sat down at the table.

"Hi, Fred. I got the deal. Mrs. Jacobs is very happy. Can I get you anything?"

"Ginny, we need to talk. How about some wine for both of us?"

"Sure, I got that nice Pinot from Gelson's that you like. I'll let you open and pour." I was too nervous.

He got the wine and glasses, opened it and poured.

"Let's just have it here around the kitchen table, like old times." That was fine with me since I was weak in the knees. My body was playing tricks on me since all of this happened.

"Ginny, a few days ago, when I said we need to talk, I was ready to leave you. Ready to give up the house and the dogs and start a new life with this young woman that I met. She was so nice and understanding and easy to talk to. And she was young and pretty and liked to do things. We used to go on long walks and find different places to have lunch. She encouraged me and I started going to the gym again. And it was great. I don't know exactly how it happened, but one day I was holding hands with her walking and we stopped at a corner and I looked at her and kissed her. She kissed me back. I almost fainted. I'm sorry to have to tell you this but we went on from there."

I didn't say anything. I didn't do anything. My hands were under the table so he couldn't see that I was squeezing them so tightly, I could feel my nails digging into my palms. I didn't trust myself to speak.

I nodded, recrossed my legs, and looked at him.

He cleared his throat, "Well it was great, she was great. I don't think I've ever been that happy. Ever. In my whole life. That's when I decided that I wanted to spend the rest of it with her. Despite the difference in our ages, despite leaving you, despite everything. I just wanted to be with her and she with me."

I still sat there, silent.

"That's when I decided to talk to you. Amy—that's her name—and I had already talked about it and she was willing. She wanted to be with me. She wanted to spend the rest of her life with me. She really wanted to be with me. So I came home and told you as quick as I could. I didn't want to hurt you."

"What happened?" I thought it was my turn to speak.

"I don't know. She didn't show up at the coffee shop that morning and I tried to call her, but there was no answer. I never knew where she lived, we always went to a hotel. She said she had a roommate. When I came back to the coffee shop in the afternoon, she had left a letter with Jack, the barista, we knew him pretty well." He stopped talking.

"What did she say? What happened?" I thought my palms were bleeding by now. I've never had this much self control.

"The note was short. She said that her mother was very sick and she needed to go home right away. She wanted to be home with her mother and she realized that she just wanted to be home. She liked me and thought that I was a great person, but she really just wanted to be home and live there. She would never be coming back to the states. Never."

My hands opened up a little. "Oh, Fred, I'm so sorry. I don't want to lose you, but I'm so sorry for you. This must have been really tough for you. How are you feeling now? Is there anything I can do?"

"I don't know. I doubt it. I'm kind of confused. I'm lost, Ginny, I'm lost."

I felt like I was melting. My heart was pounding again. I couldn't feel my hands. I crossed my legs again, just to do something.

"Is there anything I can do? I'm so sorry. I feel terrible for you." I reached out a hand to him and he took it. I didn't say anything.

We sat there like that for a while. Holding hands. My throat was dry. I wanted a sip of the Pinot, and I didn't want to stop the moment. A dog jumped up on Fred's lap and he let my hand go and started petting her.

"Fred, I know that things have been hard between us for a long time. I don't know what happened, but we stopped being an 'us.' We each went our separate ways. I know a lot of it was my fault. I'm sorry. So sorry. What are you going to do? Are you going to try and find her?"

"No Ginny, it's over. She's gone and I know it." He brushed the dog down, put his hands on the table and looked at me. By now, my heart was in my throat, but I was able to look back at him. I didn't say anything. We sat there, the two of us across the table and the two dogs on the floor.

Fred cleared his throat, shifted his position on the chair and leaned forward stretching out a hand. "Ginny, I know that this is a long shot and there's a lot of water under the bridge, but do you think, if we're careful and take care of each other, there's a shot for us?"

I didn't say anything for a long time. I looked into his eyes and they were alive and a deep blue. I realized that I hadn't looked in his eyes for quite some time. I cleared my throat and said, "Yes, I think so, maybe, yes, we might need some help, but yes." I got up and so did he and we stood holding on to each other until one of the dogs wanted to go out.

"I'll take her out," he said.

"I'll start dinner," I said.

As soon as I heard the door shut on Fred and the two dogs, as soon as I couldn't hear their steps crunching on the driveway, as soon as I could breathe again, I picked up the phone.

"Mr. Ito, here. Who's calling?"

"Mr. Ito, it's me, Mrs. Adams. You can cash that check now. The eagle has landed. I don't know who you are, or what you really do, but thank you and regards to Amy, wherever she is."

Sunday Morning

The jet screams across the sky on a quiet Sunday morning.
Silencing birds, sacred music, waking the dogs.
The noise dies.
The birds sing again, the dogs bark.
The breeze moves the shiny spider's web.

In Goshen, airplanes in the sky were an adventure.
A celebration, a silver shining bird.
We pointed, gasped and bragged about seeing it.
I dreamt of being a stewardess.

Today I brag of my cricket and mocking bird
And keep friendly with the crows that will be the last to leave.

The Beginning

As I sit here writing this, my body is drying up. I am turning to stone, one cell at a time. The process starts with my fingers and toes and works inward to my heart and brain.

I'm writing this as quickly as possible since there is no going back. Once it starts, it's irreversible. The words tumble out of my brain and into my left ear. I'm writing everything down, trying to keep up.

This hardening comes as no shock, though I thought the withering would be more gradual, a slower retreat into that good night.

But no, it's time. I'm impelled to stop, like a clock when its battery runs down. It's my time. There's no feeling left in my legs and it's harder to grasp the pen.

It doesn't feel real, but it feels right. I'm not being punished, it only feels that way. A payback for all the times I've ignored my body. Now my hands are numb.

I'm not scared. I should be, but I'm not. There's nothing to worry about. No chores, no expectations. This is what it's like, the numbness circles my waist and my breathing is shallow.

But I can still hear. I hear birds and children playing outside. It's getting dark, but slowly. The lights dim. I'm able to write only by force of will. A quick pen on smooth paper.

If this is what death is, I can take it. Drying up. Numbing out. One cell at a time. One bit of light at a time. One birdsong at a time.

Gracie

If you're stillborn, when you come into life,
can you die, since you never lived?

I named her Gracie when we got her.
She was eight weeks old.
I thought I named her after Gracie Allen—
Say goodnight, Gracie.

I know now that I named her after
my unborn, undead baby sister.
I was only two.
I'm sure I felt her moving in Mama's belly.

Mama got really big and soft.
Then she went away and didn't come home for a long time.
The baby never arrived.
Our invitation was declined.

I was moved to a house with a cat
and a blonde lady who didn't hold me.
She wasn't fat like Mama.
She left me alone.

So Gracie—that's her name—
Decided to join me.
She talks a lot, but doesn't say much.
She sleeps with me at night, every night.

Solace

I'm sitting in my small living room
that feels like the prow of a ship,
with high arched ceilings and windows.

I'm sitting on my overstuffed faded brown chair
with big soft cushions that were fluffy years ago.
I'm sitting here with my legs stretched out on the matching ottoman.
Gracie likes to climb up the ottoman onto my legs
and then over my body to the top of the chair.
She settles down on the highest cushion and the back of the chair.

She starts by looking out the window,
barking to warn me of passing cars, people, dogs, and squirrels.
Then she cuddles up, falls into the space
between the cushion and the chair
and snores into my right ear
until I awaken her for bed.

Small Things

I'm having trouble with my mind.
It jumps around and skitters,
looking for disasters and black holes,
things that go bump in the night.

I protect myself with white light,
birds, creeping fig and Gracie, the dog.
Sometimes, even people, but I find
they have lost their juice.

I sit here at my desk with the light shining down,
blue pen in my hand, purple yoga mat
rolled up in the corner. The faded yellow
rugs from Turkey on the floor.
And Gracie snoozing on the green overstuffed chair.

I sit here, comforted by small things.

October 20, 2010

Today I am grateful.
Today I am happy to be alive.
Today I am thinking old age is worth it,
this is why I grew up.

I mean, I don't want to die.
I never want to die.
So if I don't die and I grow up,
I'm going to be old
with wrinkled skin and age marks.

I just don't see any other way,
unless I become a vampire
and I can't stand the sight of blood.

Love Story

Am I pretty?
Do you love me?
Are you there for me?

That's all I want.
All I care about.
Say yes. Lie to me.

I don't care what you do.
Let's pretend.
It's only make believe.

I mail my letters in the tree in my backyard.
They're only words.
I don't care if you come.
I don't care if you see me.
I don't care anymore.
It's too late.

You're all dead.
I'm the only one left.
I'm having the last laugh,
which only you can hear.
And the fat lady's long gone.

The Demon Mirror

Sunday, April 14th, 2009, 9:44 A.M. I'm sitting in my new bedroom, at my new writing table, listening to Bach on the radio and looking out at my green garden. Some roses are coming into bloom—the Just Joey ones that I like. My resident mockingbird is singing his heart out, searching for his perfect mate. My two dogs are asleep at my feet.

The idea of things is always better than the reality of things.

I only write about people who are dead, or I can only write about people who have died for fear of hurting any living person's feelings. It's a good thing I've lived so long. I enjoy living my life and describing it or, more accurately, trying to fit it. I don't really fit my life. I look old and I feel young. I can attest to looking old when I look in the mirror.

In my bathroom are two mirrors—one on the medicine cabinet and one that is a lighted magnifying mirror used to apply makeup that I purchased on the advice of a demented decorator.

I rarely use it to apply makeup. I use it as a litmus test to see how masochistic I am at the moment of its use. I can forget about it for days and then some grumbling will come from deep inside me and challenge me to take a look. It is a modern version of Dorian Gray, except it's not in a closet. It's attached to my wall and it's electrified. It is my own personal horror show.

When I look in a regular mirror, I can see my face OK, but not really well. I have the kind of vision that just uses reading glasses. I can see the distance just fine. Close up, not so much.

So I'll go into the bathroom, let's say its morning and I'm getting ready to go to work after having taken a shower and moistened my parchment-like skin from head to toe. I brush and floss my teeth, take my vitamins—these days mostly anti-oxidants and then it's make up time, decision making time.

Do I really want to see me? Be in the now with myself? See me as others see me, assuming that most of the people that I encounter during the day will have better vision than I do? Do I want to put on my makeup using the silver-backed torture device that I introduced into my bath, or spend the day in delusion?

When I look into the medicine cabinet mirror, it's kind of a nice soft blur. Lines and sags that I'm used to. But when I look into the magnifying mirror, which is not the one that Snow White had, or maybe it is, and the Wicked Witch is staring back at me, my face looks exactly like the face in Munch's *The Scream*, only in high-def. My lines have lines and my sags have sags. I don't relate to that face at all. Why did I buy that mirror? Why do I look at it? I don't need makeup; I need a mask like in Venice at Carnival.

The prognosis is not good. It's only going to get worse. Unless I have plastic surgery, which, aside from being expensive, is difficult to endure. It will leave be with cat's eyes, a frozen expression and a gap between my face and hair.

Should I face reality or ignore it? Make believe that I'm as young as I think I am, which is around 19 most days, or start acting my chronological age?

There is the truth of the face in the medicine cabinet and the truth of the face in the magnifying mirror and the truth of the face in my head.

Meanwhile, I'm sitting here at my writing table looking out at my green garden, hearing the music and the birds. All is well. I think I'll just say, "Fuck it." After all, I can't see myself when I'm walking around or sitting here. I'll join the vampires who are quite popular today and avoid all mirrors. I'm always hated department store mirrors anyway.

Life is perfect. Thanks be to God.

A Lamentation

I have a lament. A lament. In the dictionary a lament is a formal expression of grief, an elegy or a dirge as when Will wrote "When in disgrace with fortune and men's eye, I all alone beweep my outcast state." Now I have two laments, one being that I have a lament and the other is that I can't write like Will.

I am all alone. I have no friends or only pieces of them. I have a little bit of friends, Buddha friends, writing friends, singing friends, working friends. We see only bits of each other. The little bits or reflections that we want to show at the time. As in facets of diamonds or lumps of coal.

I've lost all of my early friends. I'm not a good keeper. Maintenance is not one of my strong suits. I have trouble keeping friends. I'm always moving on or sometimes they drop me.

The truth is I like my lament more than my friends. I like life in a minor key.

I'm sitting in the platinum colored car, almost brand new, or at least it smells that way. It's my friend Georgia's car. She's driving. We've just pulled up to my house. I have my hand on the door knob to get out.

"Sarah," she says. "I have to talk to you. It's really important."

I stop getting out, settle back down on the crisp leather seat, look at Georgia, who has taken her hand off the steering wheel and has half turned to face me. She's a pretty woman with carefully bleached blonde curly hair and blue eyes, with a hint of yellow in the whites. She's petite, from Oklahoma and speaks with the hint of a drawl. She's the perfect little woman with an aura of the Fifties surrounding her.

I don't like it when someone says they have to talk to me. It's always bad news about them or me, mostly me. I take my time before turning to face her and I say:

"Georgia, what's up?"

"I can't see you anymore," she says.

"You can't see me anymore? Why? What does that mean?'

"I'm just too busy. Bob and I have a lot of social friends and I have my kids. I love you but I don't have room for you in my life any more. I'm too busy. I just don't have room for you."

She was Dear Johnning me in her car after we'd just had a nice Ladies Lunch together. This sort of thing is bad enough, but couldn't she have done it in writing, or just not answered my calls? I tried again: "Georgia, is it something I've done or said? Are you angry or upset about something?"

"No. I just don't have room for you anymore. I love you, but I'm too busy for you."

It was a personal, special delivery, Dear John note in front of my own home. I still didn't get out.

Georgia was a nice woman, a good housekeeper. She gave wonderful parties. She was the ideal "little woman." I used to play bridge and tennis with her husband before we met. I hadn't seen a lot of her lately, we used to play ladies doubles and go to occasional tennis matches together and even played doubles once with our daughters. I never thought we were that close.

"Georgia, I'm really sorry. I'll miss you and Bob," I said. I almost said "be well and prosper," but I didn't and got out of the car and went into my house.

I got in the house and sat down in my favorite chair and Joey jumped on my lap. And thought about what I'd be missing. Not the parties. I always drink or eat too much, and I never went to her annual cookie party wherein you bake twelve cookies and then share them and the recipe with others. That party would have been some kind of hell for me. I would have had to turn down dozens of cookies. And we hadn't been seeing that much of each other since she'd moved, anyway.

I really wasn't missing much. It just felt weird to be dumped like that. Atrophy would have suited me just fine.

As I look back on this scene, this living Dear John letter, I've decided that this was probably one of the kindest and nicest things that anyone has ever said to me. She didn't have room for me in her life. The truth is I don't have room for me either. I'm too much to handle. I'm too sensitive and I complain all the time. Nothing is quite right. My imagination is much better than my reality. I love thinking of things more than just doing them. It's like when I was a kid and read the Sears and Monkey Wards catalogues and imagined all the toys and cowgirl costumes I could buy.

I'm working on a lower maintenance, more active model of myself. I'd be happy to trade myself in, but if the new model is worse, then what?

Lovers

They're all dead.
My lovers are all dead.
The big man from New Haven,
The little guy from New Jersey.
The olive-skinned one from New York.

They're all gone. No more looks of love.
No hands to hold.
No feeling their heartbeat pressed against me.
No smelling their skin.
No more hearing their breathing.
It's all gone.

Except, except for me.
I am the keeper. The note-taker.
They're not here, not next to me,
but I remember them all. Their taste.
The smell of their breath.
And their eyes. I don't forget their eyes.

Last Lover Poem

She's on the red dining room table
looking out the window,
watching for people, cars and dogs,
guarding her territory.

The little dog that snores
And comforts me at night
when I feel her body pressed against my leg,
the little dog who keeps me alive and warm.

Joining the Orange Butterfly

I feel the music in my right foot.
The orange butterfly roams the green yard,
and the dry wind shakes the leaves.

Were I to die right now,
this very moment.
I would be complete,
content "as with marrow and fatness."

The wind is getting stronger,
and the white flowers on the vine dance.
The house creaks, wanting to join with the wind.

I am with them in my mind for now,
but someday I shall join them.

A Weekday Morning

My garden calls to me.
It is mostly green: the creeping fig,
the grass, the flowerless rose bushes.
The only color from the red crown of thorns.

My garden calls to me and wants me to stay
and feel the breeze on my face
and hear the children playing in the background
and the planes overhead.

I can't stay with my garden.
I have to work.
I have to be with people. Hear them talk.
People are not green.

Someday, I will be part of the garden
as my husband is now.
Someday, I won't have to listen to other's words.
Someday, I'll just be.
Someday.

A Walk in the Fog

The man wearing a gray shirt
was standing on the walking path facing me.
It was a still, foggy, gray morning,
even the crows were silent.
He had his arms stretched out parallel to the ground.
He stood there and didn't move.
It was as if he was on the deck of a carrier ship,
waiting for a signal
and I was waiting for his direction
to know when to move.
I couldn't see his face.
All I could see was this slim,
gray figure, looking straight ahead.
The fog broke and the sun came out
shining on his head, casting sharp shadows.
He still didn't move and neither did I.
There was a message for me. I knew it.
The crows started jabbering
and a squirrel ran out of the bushes
and up a tree.
The man folded his shape into a straight line,
turned around
and walked away.
Today wasn't my day.

A Strange Day

It's a strange day, a beautiful one here
One day post rain, when everything is clean and sparkles.
The green in my garden is lighter, the few red flowers brighter.
All this gaiety overwhelms me.

Does anyone have the right to celebrate?
What about Haiti and the real estate market?
What about jobs and foreclosures?

We all know that Damocles' sword still hangs above our heads.
We all know that the Fates are restless.
We all know the end is near.

There are so many ways that the end will come.
Fire, flood, pestilence, nuclear, anthrax.
and we're worried that we don't have enough
ways to kill ourselves so we keep making them up.
There's always room for one more way with great rewards.

I guess I'll have to put up with this clear, bright sunshine,
and try not to kill myself in my car.

A Blue Moon Day

Am I Lazarus? Have I risen from the dead yet? I think not. I'm not ready to come back. When I'm dead I'm wrapped in gauze or Saran Wrap. There's a space between me and thee, which I find comforting.

I don't have to take care of myself or anyone else. I don't have to diet, exercise, read, write. No more searching for words or looking at people's faces for reactions. I don't have to please anybody, even myself.

The big question when returning from the dead is how have they gotten along without me? I'm afraid it will be "Quite well, thank you." Or, "You were dead? I had no idea." The most devastating cut of all. And what of my possessions—the watch that I wear every day, my rings, the flannel pajamas that I love. Where have they gone? Can I live without them? There are so many problems to be solved on returning to life: bills to be paid, obligations to be met, words to be found.

There are good things in life, too: the first pee in the morning, the sound of the tea kettle and early morning Baroque. My time, before anyone but the birds are up.

Joey's at my feet, his hind legs spread out and his back flat, head down, his whole brown and white Jack Russell body resting on the fake Persian carpet. He'll stay there until I get up and then follow me around the house.

I guess I'll have to stay alive so that Joey will know where to go.

A Happening

The brillig sun careened into my heart and caused a riotous explosion. It was jammed with creatures that had lain dormant these many years.

Rapunzel was still fighting with Rumpelstiltskin. Piglet was trying to cheer up Eeyore, and Pinocchio was in the middle of a long story but no one was listening because who could believe him?

The Red Queen was there still being her imperious best, shouting orders accompanied by the most royal of gestures. Sleeping Beauty was just getting over chronic fatigue syndrome and Snow White was getting a facial. Prince Charming was there as well, looking handsome and doing nothing.

The Owl and the Pussycat were having tea with the Cheshire Cat and they were all using runcible spoons. Everyone seemed very busy, except for the Prince, of course. Pooh and Christopher Robin were going to investigate heffalumps.

We knocked around my heart for the longest of times, eons and eons. It was a complex and complicated chamber of activities. I did also manage to see the Snow Queen and the Pied Piper who could find no rats but plenty of children.

The Little Prince came and took me to the moon and stars. He took me to the Pleiades, Andromeda, Pegasus and Hercules. We sat on Aries, played some games with Ursa Minor and sipped chamomile tea with Cassiopeia. At which point, thanks to the Prince's generous and courtly invitation, I decided to stay. The words are prettier here.

By Heart

Two women talked last night.
Two women well past a certain age.
They spoke of their friendship, husbands and children,
the life that each had lived.
One cried for the loss of her father to the second wife.
The other sang of her love of God.
I sat with the other women in the room
knowing their stories by heart.

During a Meditation

My world is very small.
Peopled with women, friends and lovers.
Each one looks at me and I look at them.
Judging, sorting, placing.
This or that. Up or down.
What do we think, you or I,
how do we fit in?
Good or bad?
Right or wrong?
Our thoughts are chasms.
Can we leap over them to the other?

Only in the silence.

Failed Promises

My life is full of failed promises.

I told my husband I would never leave him,
and I did.

I told my husband I would always be faithful,
and I wasn't

I told my husband I'd give myself completely to him,
and I didn't

It's as if as soon as I promise something,
the other me says no.

So when I'm with you,
don't listen to me.

I want to be the person I am in my own mind.
I want to be someone I'm not.

My Muse

Sharon Olds, you can go fuck yourself.
You can take your long aristocratic head
with your stringy black hair
and put it up your elegant greedy vagina.

You can stick your tumescent tongue
in up to your cretinous cervix
and lick to your heart's content.
At the last moment, you can
excrete venomous bile
out of your dark, dank orifice.

I am sick of you.
Sick of your gelatinous, slimy images.
Oozing out of disgusting organisms.
Everything covered with jism.

Get me out of your subconscious.
I want nothing of your dreams.
Give me a hard-ass muse.
You're no fun.

I can't begin to imitate your images.
Everything I come up with is second rate.
You're a skinny-ass bitch of a muse
leading an elegant life on the
Upper West Side and the Hamptons.

I want to go back to my simple life.
I want to stop opening every vein.
I've lived with my ghosts for too long.
You might be a great poet,
but you're a lousy muse.

You're fired.

Rimbaud Squared

Gleaming snails of brown ornaments disturbed the rhythm of the puree windstorm that opened the sealed mouth of the grotesque breast of the ancient chimera screaming in the blue. Billy wanted chocolate milk this time. Great daffodils blew away my headache and worried the harvesting of black beads from the shores of my eyes.

No, that won't do. It's not right, too wrinkly. Squizzled up in the morning dream. Screaming raunchy armpits into the blue of the day. Sitting stones move up and down. It's time to change the time. Way to do this before the after. Much need that chunk of ground brown-red hand for sale at Gelson's, or was it Whole Foods?

Numbers rule. Forty-three is good or was it 29? Gasping strands of wire entangle my hands so that the mix of azure blue transposed into the brain of a newt turns into the red light at the street corner. Those teeth laugh at me on the table and move into my left ear and I lie down in blue waters and sleep into the space between my eyes.

The llama calls for me and I walk into the wall of gleaming iron. The busted lady bends over and globules of wet dirt fall out and I find the baby from long ago who has painted feet and green gills. There's also an overdue Verizon bill standing trenchant on the rim of granules of kittens. Makers do it. The contamination of gaseous masses runs triumphant through the grass.

My Mind

Brains full of snakes writhing in a crazy rhythm,
boa constrictors, asps, king cobras,
all hissing their curses.

Nightmares personified.
Jarring my sensory equipment.

I'm too frightened to be hysterical.
There is no room to maneuver.
I have done it this time.
I will succumb, submit to my fate.
If only they were puppies.

The birds jabber nonstop.
Crows caw in my brain
babble, rattle, chatter: it's a party in there with needless noise.

They're in my left ear now,
jammed against my brain.
No nightingales, no mockingbirds, no canaries.
Just jawing prophets of this century,
ludicrous in their phony self importance.

Potential

I always want everything to be perfect, absolutely perfect. That's why writing is so hard. I want each word on the paper to stand on its own, to rise up, be counted, to be precise, expressive of my every thought with layers of meaning attached.

I'm making myself sick with all these words—they're useless, banal, dull—just dripping off my pen at will—I'm out of control.

What I'd like is for everything to be undone, unmade, unwritten—in the future—not here yet, full of potential like the pregnant pause. It's like entering a room for the first time or seeing a movie for the first time. I like the ideas of things more that the things themselves

Furniture gets dusty, movies turn out to be bad, people get old, babies cry. I like to think about all these things without having to deal with them. I want to live in a world that isn't here yet. A world full of potential—good things just around the corner, ships coming in—a world full of puppies, kittens, blank sheets of paper—a world full of opening days, seedlings, sprouts, first notes, first glances, early dawn, birdsong.

I like ideas, dreams, hope, rehearsal dinners, thresholds, roads not yet crossed. In such a world I can dream of happy endings, true love, masterpieces, miracles.

But today, right now, I have to put my pen away, take a shower, get dressed, put makeup on and go out and face the people I'll run into today. That's my life here and now.

And tomorrow? Tomorrow I'll have to read this.

A Friday in January

The morning sun is shining on my French doors,
and I can see the cleaning marks on some of the panes.
I can see my little garden, mostly green right now.
The creeping fig on the garage wall, the pruned rose bushes,
the brown dirt, the small green lawn.
It is asleep.

Except, except for two plants in terra cotta containers.
They have thick, rough, light-gray stems,
green leaves and bright red flowers,
bringing Christmas to my garden.
Bringing thoughts of good things to come.
They're perky, stalwart,
optimistic and awake.

Sentinels of goodness,
like my two dogs.

Valentine's Day 2011

I woke up this morning hearing the crows
scrabble across the roof.
One of them pecked at my skylight.

I got up and looked out the French doors.
The sun was just coming up,
backlighting my garden.

The sky was blue with white clouds.
And the mockingbird was on top of the telephone pole,
singing his morning prayers.

The Garden

It's late afternoon. The sky has clouded up
and the breeze is coming from the west
and it's a little cold.

The leaves of the trees rustle as the wind comes up.
Some distant chimes ring out.
I feel the wind in my face. It's cold. It lifts my hair.

The wind comes from the far west,
touches me and then leaves.
A small plane flies across the sky
to the west against the wind.

The birds are quiet for the moment.
A woman is talking to her child.
How much longer? How many more hours
will I have to sit here and listen to the leaves
and hear the woman talk?

A jet races across the sky.
Noisy, rough, angry, a bully.

My hand gets cold and I cannot leave.
I cannot stop. I have nowhere to go.
Nothing matters but the wind.
Where is it going? Where am I?

The leaves rustle, the birds sing
and the mother calls to her child.

But for me it will never be the same. Never.
A moment like this with the black ink marking the page.
My feet and hands chilled.
A dog barks. Another plane comes over the hill.

I have nothing to say. Nothing to do.
I can feel the earth moving and hear the wind in the trees.
They still stand.
I still sit.
The wind is very cold.
I haven't fallen off.

The Whole Truth

I fell in love with sensitivity training as soon as I heard about it. The idea was that we'd all get together in groups, listen to each other, empathize, do a lot of active listening, and we'd come out better humans. So I arranged for a weekend away from the kids and my husband and went down to La Jolla for a three-day meeting, sponsored by the Carl Rogers Institute. Rogers was the father of client-centered therapy.

There were twelve of us in our group, including a couple of forest rangers. As we talked and listened to each other's lives, there was one guy that I really liked. He was a Catholic parish priest from Detroit. He was good looking, with a high forehead that seemed intelligent, rather than foreshadowing baldness, and had short brown hair, unusual in the late sixties. He wasn't dressed in his collar, so I didn't learn his profession until the second day.

We had coffee together during the breaks, and went out with a group for dinner on Saturday night. On Sunday, the last day, I asked him what his plans were: "I'm scheduled for a retreat in San Diego and I have some time to kill before that. I'm planning to just drive around Southern California and get to know it."

"Come up and stay with me and Bob and the kids for a couple of days. We'd love to have you and you can have the den." I loved Larry and I was sure that Bob would like him too.

Larry arrived the following Monday. He was good with the kids and even got on well with the dog and the cat. Bob would be the final test.

Bob got home at six and everything went fine. Both Larry and Bob were liberal, against the war, and loved to talk politics. My chicken casserole came out OK and the kids were great. We put them to bed and stayed up and chatted, drank some wine and went to bed.

The next day was a big day for Larry, me and the kids. It turned out that Larry liked to fish and we went out fishing in a boat that left the Marina early in the morning. It was a beautiful day. Larry baited the kids' hooks, the kids caught some fish, and there were plenty of donuts. We came home exhausted.

Dinner that night was fresh fish. The kids were exuberant and couldn't stop talking of their day. They had really bonded with Larry. After dinner we had some wine, talked of the day until Bob got sick of it and then the talk turned to politics.

Larry did say a little more about his background. He came from a suburb of Detroit, was the oldest of four children, went to seminary right after high school, and had been an ordained priest for about three years. I was tired and Bob had to get up early for work, so we both went to bed around 10:30. Larry stayed up to read.

In the middle of the night—it seemed like the middle—someone was knocking on our bedroom door. At first, I didn't know who it was. One of the kids would have come in, crying. It had to be Larry.

"Come in," I said.

"Sarah, I have to talk to you and Bob," said Larry.

"He's still asleep. I'll just get up and come," I said.

"No, I have to talk to Bob, too. It's really important. Please, I hate to bother you. Please."

"OK, I'll get him up." I nudged Bob as gently as possible. We threw on our robes, and stumbled out to the living room. I was curious and Bob was annoyed.

Larry had left some lights on in the living room and was sitting in the Lincoln Rocker so Bob and I sat down on our blue couch, facing him.

"Well Larry, what is it? What's going on? What's so important that we both had to get up? Can we help?" I said in my most compassionate voice.

"I have to tell you something that I've never told anyone before. It's really important. Thanks for listening," he said.

Bob gave me one of those glances that said "look what you've gotten us into now." He got up and went to the kitchen for a glass of water.

"I need to talk to both of you. Please."

So Bob came back and plopped down on the couch, glass in hand, "What's up? "He said, "I'm tired."

"This is something I've never shared with anyone and I have to tell someone now. I have to."

"OK, tell us. We're listening," I said in my most empathetic voice.

I put my hand on Bob's to keep him on the couch. I knew he was ready to go back to bed.

"I'm a homosexual. I've never told anyone."

I didn't know what to say. I felt that I have to say something. The right word. The most compassionate empathetic response. I knew Bob wasn't going to say anything.

"So you're a homosexual. That's OK. Do you want to talk about it some more? Are you sure? Is there anything we can do to help?" I was starting to babble. I had had a lot of gay friends in New York and so had Bob. We weren't completely unaware, even here in Orange County. "How can we help?" I repeated.

"Sarah," he said. "I'm attracted to your husband."

"That's nice," I said. "I think he's good looking too."

Bob was silent.

"Listen Sarah, I'm attracted to your husband, sexually," he repeated.

It was one o'clock in the morning and here was this man sitting across from me, in my living room, saying that he was attracted to my husband. I knew I was supposed to say something, and I was clueless. Bob was in a stupor.

"Are you sure?" I finally said.

"Sarah, when I look at your husband, I get a hard-on. I'm sure."

Well there was nothing I could say to that. I'd never even thought about Larry's penis, much less his erected one. I was out of my league.

"Well, I'm not attracted to you," said Bob. He walked out and went to bed.

I sat there for a few minutes; trying to think of a compassionate response at one in the morning, something like "Do you still have the erection now? How does it feel? Do you have one often?" I couldn't say anything more. I struck out. Nothing came to mind. Nothing.

I told Larry I'd see him in the morning.

The next morning Bob got up and left for work early as planned. I made a good breakfast for Larry and the kids.

When the kids went out to play, Larry said he'd be taking off and was already packed. He said goodbye to the kids, got in his car and drove off. I wished him safe travels.

After he left, I sat down at my kitchen table and thought. Here is the one time in my life when someone I knew told me something that was true and I didn't know how to deal with it, or even if I should be dealing with it. It was time to resign my position as The Sovereign of Sensitivity, The Queen of Compassion and The Empress of Empathy. So much for the truth. I knew that I would never forget Larry, his attraction to my husband, and his erect penis.

The Whole Truth 203

The Showing

I was in the Palisades at my new listing waiting for the agent to show with her client. They were late. I called her on her cell and they were lost. She kept asking if the unit was on the right or left side of the street. "If you're going up the hill," I said, "it's on the left side. If you're going down the hill it's on the right," She didn't get it and I heard this booming voice telling her to turn around. The voice was so loud, she couldn't hear me.

"I'll come out and get you," I said. "I'll stand on the street and you'll see me."

She was still talking and the voice was giving commands as I hung up.

I went out and they had just pulled up in a new white BMW. The agent, a tall slim blonde, got out and yelled at the top of her voice: "We're here, I told you so. You got me confused." She was yelling at her passenger. He got out, lumbered around the front of the car and crossed the street. He was a big man. He was wearing tan shorts and his legs were bowed and there were dark blotches decorating each leg. I could hear his breathing as he approached.

"I told her where to go," he said in a loud voice. "We're here. Isn't this nice,"

I showed them the way to the townhouse. I walked slowly to accommodate him.

When we entered, he said, "Can I use the bathroom?"

"Of course," I said. "There's a guest bath up the steps." I pointed to it and he lumbered up the five steps. His breathing was getting louder and creaky. The agent and I waited in the entry so that we could show him the whole house. I looked at her and said, "Is he OK? He seems to be having a hard time getting around. You know that this is a townhouse with a lot of steps."

"Oh yes. He's fine. He's used to steps." She had a slight accent.

He came out and we proceeded with the showing. He was still breathing heavily and announcing the function of each room. THE LIVING ROOM. THE BATHROOM.

He took a long time over THE BIDET. And he commented on my client's clothing, shoes, toiletry, etc. The agent kept saying how nice and bright it was and telling him to look at the windows because it was an end unit. I trailed along hoping that nothing got broken and that I wouldn't have to do CPR. His breathing was still loud.

We walked downstairs, back to the entrance, and I said, "The garage is down below. Maybe you'd like to see it on your next visit?"

"No," he bellowed. "Let's see it now." He was quite jolly and enjoying the showing.

I let his agent lead the way downstairs, figuring that he could fall on her and I'd be free to call 911. We dragged ourselves back upstairs after noticing the washer/dryer and extra storage. At the entrance I turned to him and said, "Do you have any questions?"

"Yes," he said, "Can I use the bathroom again?"

"Of course, you know where it is."

He hung on the railing and went up the stairs to the next level, went inside and closed the door. The agent and I chatted about Malibu—she lived and worked there. Then we noted the weather, which was changing. We were running out of small talk, "He's been in there a long time," I said. "Do you think he died?"

"No," she giggled. "He's fine."

"This is a townhouse—a three level flat. Why did you bring him here?"

"Oh he lives on Coastline, with a lot of steps. He's renting. He wants to buy a place."

We waited. I noticed that she was a real blonde and was in great shape, thin but not skinny. Her arms were muscular. She wore tight brown leggings on her sculptured legs. She never stood still and started tapping her right foot. She was wearing gold sandals.

The door opened and he came out. "Ilse," he said, "there's a problem. I've blocked the toilet. It won't flush."

"Did you flush it again?"

"Yes. I've tried it a few times."

We walked up the stairs. She was ahead of me. He came out and sat on one of the chairs.

"You probably used too much toilet paper. I'll take care of it," said Ilse.

I followed her to the bathroom and stood at the door watching her. She lifted the lid of the toilet. Her faced changed, her eyes widened and her jaw snapped shut. Whatever was in there was not good.

"I'll take care of it," she repeated. She walked out of the bathroom and said, "We can't leave her like this" (meaning me, thank God). She walked around the kitchen a bit, her gold sandals clacking on the floor. "I'm

German. I can take care of anything. I need a basket. I need something to hold water." She looked around and found a trash can in the bathroom, went to the kitchen, filled it up with water and went back into the bathroom. She did this twice.

"Got it," she said. "It's fine. He used too much toilet paper. I'm German and I live in Malibu. I can take care of this."

The client smiled, got up from his chair and walked down the stairs.

"Thank you very much, it's a great place," he said.

"He has bathroom problems," she whispered to me.

"Would you like to see the pool and gym area" I said.

"No. We'll see that next time," as they walked down the lane. He was telling her something at the top of his voice and she was leading the way looking straight ahead.

I shut the front door went back to the bathroom. Opened the door to the bathroom and looked down at the toilet, afraid of what I might see. When I was a kid I used to be scared of snakes hanging out there. What if she hadn't really fixed it and there was something lingering? Something alive? I didn't like the look on her face when she saw it. I opened the lid and looked down.

There was nothing there, only water and at the right level. I flushed it again and it was fine. I closed the lid. That's what good real estate agents do. I left the house singing "*Du, du liebst mir in herzen.*" The gods had saved me again.

Storage

The creeping fig has been tamed for now.
Gracie is snoring on the bed
and Mozart's on the FM.

I measure my life
by words on the page,
looking for words
that I have forgotten.

And words that I have ignored,
left behind, entombed.
People words, name words,
family words—they're all gone.

These are the words
stored in my body,
owned by me.
I am their keeper.

Palliative

Palliative, what a pretty word.
It rolls around the tongue.
It sounds luscious, liquid and lovely.
Palliative, make nice, make smooth, make calm.

Palliative care until death.
No. Not for me.
I'll have none of that.
I don't want any trumped up ride.
Any fogged up view.
No cheese cloth over the camera for me.

I want to be there. All of me.
Scared to death.
But not scared out of my wits.

I want to be the last decision maker.
I want to have the last trump card,
but that may not be up to me.
It may not be graceful, or blessed, or quiet,
but at least the next-to-the last moment will be mine.

My Table

I am surrounded by pieces of my life:
the remote for my music,
a coaster for my hot tea,
the necklace I took off last night.
a notebook for my dreams—that's pretty empty—
the phone and this pad, my pens in the drawer.

I also have two dogs nearby—Gracie's snoring.
That's it—my life on the table—did I mention the gray phone?
And I forgot the bright-colored sticky pad.

I put these things there and I'm responsible for them.
They all have meaning to me.
When I die and a stranger comes, she'll sweep them away:
my dreams, my notes, the odd coaster.
It'll take less than five minutes, and I'll be gone.

Home

I left on a journey when I was young and kept losing things, like my right eye. I thought it was on my face and I looked in a mirror that I found on the road and it was gone—it wasn't anywhere on my body, not on my stomach and not on my hand or my foot. It had drained away in a stream of blue, white, and black gelatinous mass. I thought that maybe if I ate something really bad, like that green frog at the edge of the infected lake, or the brown and white caterpillar that I had just stepped on, my eye would come back, and it never did.

I decided to cut off my face and only look at the left side. I did this because my right side was too stupid to keep its own eye. It couldn't be trusted. My right arm was messed up too. How am I going to climb Mount Everest?

I am always losing blood too—red blood, brown blood, thick blood, dripping blood, with chunks of black. The blood comes from my every orifice, my nose, my mouth, my eyes, my vagina, draining, dripping, running, oozing down my face. It falls into a puddle at my feet. I can step into it and feel it, and run my toes thru it, and as I walk out of the puddle and turn around, I can see my bloody footprints.

Foolish girl—I thought that growing up I would find these things and grow another eye in the center of my head maybe and the blood would stop oozing and my hair would turn blonde as the sun and my teeth would gleam bright as a searchlight on a dark night and life would be rosey/posey without thorns. And I thought that the mountain was a gentle slope with a clear path and the only animals were friendly—there was not a gnome or a troll to be found.

Instead my feet are shredded and torn and the nights are full of banshees and gnomes and cries from chained children screaming for mama. Their noise gets into my head so bad that I can't hear anything else. I'm looking for the ocean because that will heal me and clean the blood and the snot. The waves make a good noise—no more screams and I can't find them. The sea isn't in the mountains. I roll down the hill because it's faster and as I spin, I find a lake with a huge fish. He tells me he'll take me to the ocean and I believe him, but he stinks of a fish store, that dead fish smell. The smell of the rotting grave of fishes, the smell that you can't wash off your hands. Even Ivory Soap—the 99% pure stuff—can't wash it off.

I run from the fish and use my nose. I sniff and smell and inhale and under everything, under the smell of cars, cats and people and shit and perfume and rage and greed, under all that I get a sniff. It's wet and clean and every sniff is different and it's familiar, it's home, it runs through my body and lets me know that I will be home, all of me.

I walk and walk and walk and then I feel with my feet, the sand. The sand welcomes me. The sand gives way to me. The sand shapes my feet and embraces each step. I walk slower now. The waves are louder and I climb to get to them. I come down the sand hill to wet sand, and my feet sink deeper and deeper and I stop to let the sea run through my feet, and I turn and look at my footprints in the sand. They are there and they are leaving at the same time. I go deeper in the water and it is good. Both feet feel good, cold and alive and wet. I sit down so my bottom can get wet. I stay seated and the wave comes and I am all wet and I am clean and I smell of the sea, I smell of the sea and all good things. I smell of the sea and the shit and snot and blood are gone. There is only the sea and me. Just us. Me and the sea. And it's right. No screaming children. No mirrors. No right side. Just me and the sea and I am home.

www.ingramcontent.com/pod-product-compliance
Lightning Source LLC
Chambersburg PA
CBHW022127080426
42734CB00006B/260